The Mini Minimalist
Pizza, Pasta & Grains

Mark Bittman

Bittman

The Mini Minimalist

Pizza, Pasta & Grains

Clarkson Potter/Publishers
New York

Contents

Pizza

Pizza Dough

People can never seem to get enough pizza, and how many a pizza will serve depends on the heartiness of the toppings, the thickness of the crust, and whether you're serving anything along with it. But I've found generally that this dough recipe will make two twelve- or thirteen-inch pizzas.

Makes: Two 12- to 13-inch pies, enough for 4 people

Time: 1 hour or more

3 cups all-purpose or bread flour, plus more as needed

2 teaspoons instant yeast

2 teaspoons coarse kosher or sea salt, plus extra for sprinkling

2 tablespoons extra virgin olive oil

1. Combine the flour, yeast, and salt in a food processor. Turn the machine on and add 1 cup of warm water and the oil through the feed tube.

2. Process for about 30 seconds, adding more water, a little at a time, until the mixture forms a ball and is slightly sticky to the touch. If it is dry, add another tablespoon or two of water and process for another 10 seconds. (In the unlikely event that the mixture is too sticky, add flour, a tablespoon at a time.)

3. Turn the dough onto a floured work surface and knead by hand for a few seconds to form a smooth, round ball. Put the dough in a bowl and cover with plastic wrap; let rise until the dough doubles in size, 1 to 2 hours. (You can cut this rising time short if you are in a hurry, or you can let the dough rise more slowly, in the refrigerator, for 6 to 8 hours.) Proceed to step 4, or wrap the dough tightly in plastic and freeze for up to a month. (Defrost in a covered bowl in the refrigerator or at room temperature.)

4. When the dough is ready, form it into a ball; divide it into 2 or more pieces if you like, rolling each piece into a ball. Put each ball on a lightly floured surface, sprinkle with a little flour, and cover with plastic wrap or a towel. Let rest until they puff slightly, about 20 minutes. Proceed with any of the recipes that follow.

Wine: Chianti or another rough red is usually best.

Serving: Roasted Red Peppers (Vegetables, page 58), Simple Green Salad (Vegetables, page 10), and/or Tomato Salad with Basil (Vegetables, page 20)

Pizza with Four Cheeses and Basil

Makes: 2 to 4 servings

Time: 30 minutes (with premade dough)

1 recipe Pizza Dough (page 8)

Olive oil as needed

½ cup shredded or cubed mozzarella cheese

½ cup shredded or cubed Fontina or Taleggio cheese

½ cup freshly grated Pecorino Romano cheese

½ cup freshly grated Parmigiano-Reggiano cheese

½ cup coarsely chopped or torn fresh basil

1. For grilled pizza, start a charcoal or wood fire, or preheat a gas grill to the maximum. Roll or lightly press each dough ball into a flat round, lightly flouring the work surface and the dough as necessary (do not use more flour than you need to). Let the rounds sit for a few minutes, then roll or pat out the dough, as thinly as you like, turning occasionally and sprinkling the top with flour as necessary.

   For baked pizza, preheat the oven to 500°F. Oil one or more baking sheets, then press each dough ball into a flat round directly on the oiled sheet(s). Pat out the dough, as thinly as you like, oiling your hands if necessary. Or, if you have a baking stone, put it in the oven while preheating, then roll or pat out the dough as for grilled pizza, putting it on a peel to transfer it to the oven..

2. To grill the pizza, slide it directly onto the grill. Cook until brown grill marks appear, 3 to 5 minutes, depending on your grill heat. Turn with a spatula or tongs, then top with the cheeses and basil. Cover the grill and cook until the bottom is crisp and brown and the cheeses are melted, 5 to 10 minutes.

To bake the pizza, top with the cheeses, slide the baking sheet into the oven (or the pizza itself onto the stone), and bake for about 10 minutes, or until nearly done. Sprinkle with the basil and finish baking, a few more minutes.

Wine: Chianti or another rough red is usually best.

Serving: Roasted Red Peppers (Vegetables, page 58), Simple Green Salad (Vegetables, page 10), and/or Tomato Salad with Basil (Vegetables, page 20)

Pizza with Green Tomatoes

Makes: 2 to 4 servings

Time: 40 to 50 minutes (with premade dough)

1 recipe Pizza Dough (page 8)

Olive oil as needed

2 large or 4 small green tomatoes

1 cup freshly grated Parmigiano-Reggiano cheese

½ cup coarsely chopped or torn fresh basil

1. For grilled pizza, start a medium-hot charcoal or wood fire, or preheat a gas grill to the maximum. Roll or lightly press each dough ball into a flat round, lightly flouring the work surface and the dough as necessary (do not use more flour than you need to). Let the rounds sit for a few minutes, then roll or pat out the dough, as thinly as you like, turning occasionally and sprinkling the top with flour as necessary.

   For baked pizza, preheat the oven to 500°F. Oil one or more baking sheets, then press each dough ball into a flat round directly on the oiled sheet(s). Pat out the dough, as thinly as you like, oiling your hands if necessary. Or, if you have a baking stone, put it in the oven while preheating, then roll or pat out the dough as for grilled pizza, putting it on a peel to transfer it to the oven.

2. Core and thinly slice the tomatoes. Salt the slices lightly and let them sit for at least 20 minutes, then drain off any accumulated liquid.

3. To grill the pizza, slide it directly onto the grill. Cook until brown grill marks appear, 3 to 5 minutes, depending on your grill heat. Turn with a spatula or tongs, then top with the tomatoes, cheese, and basil. Cover the grill and cook until the bottom is crisp and brown and the cheese is melted, 5 to 10 minutes.

To bake the pizza, top with the tomatoes and cheese, slide the baking sheet into the oven (or the pizza itself onto the stone), and bake for about 10 minutes, or until nearly done. Sprinkle with the basil and finish baking, a few more minutes.

Wine: Chianti or another rough red is usually best.

Serving: Roasted Red Peppers (Vegetables, page 58), Simple Green Salad (Vegetables, page 10), and/or Tomato Salad with Basil (Vegetables, page 20)

Pizza with Tomatoes, Onions, and Olives

Makes: 2 to 4 servings

Time: 35 minutes (with premade dough)

1 recipe Pizza Dough (page 8)

4 or 5 ripe tomatoes

Coarse salt

1 medium red onion or 4 shallots, chopped

20 black olives, such as kalamata or oil-cured, pitted and chopped

Olive oil as needed

1. For grilled pizza, start a medium-hot charcoal or wood fire or preheat a gas grill to the maximum. Roll or lightly press each dough ball into a flat round, lightly flouring the work surface and the dough as necessary (do not use more flour than you need to). Let the rounds sit for a few minutes, then roll or pat out the dough, as thinly as you like, turning occasionally and sprinkling the top with flour as necessary.

   For baked pizza, preheat the oven to 500°F. Oil one or more baking sheets, then press each dough ball into a flat round directly on the oiled sheet(s). Pat out the dough, as thinly as you like, oiling your hands if necessary. Or, if you have a baking stone, put it in the oven while preheating, then roll or pat out the dough as for grilled pizza, putting it on a peel to transfer it to the oven.

2. Meanwhile, core the tomatoes, cut them in half horizontally, and gently squeeze out the liquid and most of the seeds. Slice as thinly as possible, lightly salt, and let the slices sit for at least 20 minutes. Drain off any excess liquid.

3. To grill the pizza, slide it directly onto the grill. Cook until brown grill marks appear, 3 to 5 minutes, depending on your grill heat. Turn with a spatula or tongs, top with the tomatoes, onion, and olives, and drizzle with olive oil. Cover the grill and cook until the bottom is crisp and brown and the tomatoes hot, 7 to 10 minutes.

To bake the pizza, top with the tomatoes, onion, olives, and a little olive oil, slide the baking sheet into the oven (or the pizza itself onto the stone), and bake for about 15 minutes, depending on the oven heat, or until nicely browned.

Wine: Chianti or another rough red is usually best.

Serving: Roasted Red Peppers (Vegetables, page 58), Simple Green Salad (Vegetables, page 10), and/or Tomato Salad with Basil (Vegetables, page 20)

Pizza with Zucchini and Sausage

Makes: 2 to 4 servings

Time: 45 minutes (with premade dough)

1 recipe Pizza Dough (page 8)

4 small or 2 medium zucchini

Coarse salt

2 or 3 sweet Italian sausages, meat removed from the casing and crumbled

2 teaspoons minced garlic

Olive oil as needed

1. For grilled pizza, start a medium-hot charcoal or wood fire or preheat a gas grill to the maximum. Roll or lightly press each dough ball into a flat round, lightly flouring the work surface and the dough as necessary (do not use more flour than you need to). Let the rounds sit for a few minutes, then roll or pat out the dough, as thinly as you like, turning occasionally and sprinkling the top with flour as necessary.

   For baked pizza, preheat the oven to 500°F. Oil one or more baking sheets, then press each dough ball into a flat round directly on the oiled sheet(s). Pat out the dough, as thinly as you like, oiling your hands if necessary. Or, if you have a baking stone, put it in the oven while preheating, then roll or pat out the dough as for grilled pizza, putting it on a peel to transfer it to the oven.

2. Meanwhile, thinly slice the zucchini. Salt the slices lightly and let them sit for at least 20 minutes, then drain off any accumulated liquid.

3. To grill the pizza, slide it directly onto the grill. Cook until brown grill marks appear, 3 to 5 minutes, depending on your grill heat. Turn with a spatula or tongs, then top with the zucchini, sausage, and garlic. Cover the grill and cook until the bottom is crisp and brown and the sausage cooked through, 7 to 10 minutes.

   To bake the pizza, top with the zucchini, sausage, and garlic, slide the baking sheet into the oven (or the pizza itself onto the stone), and bake for about 15 minutes, depending on the oven heat, or until nicely browned and the sausage is cooked through.

Wine: Chianti or another rough red is usually best.

Serving: Roasted Red Peppers (Vegetables, page 58), Simple Green Salad (Vegetables, page 10), and/or Tomato Salad with Basil (Vegetables, page 20)

Pizza with Arugula, Corn, and Bacon

Makes: 2 to 4 servings

Time: 40 to 50 minutes (with premade dough)

---

1 recipe Pizza Dough (page 8)

Olive oil as needed

6 cups loosely packed washed, dried, and shredded arugula

Kernels from 4 ears corn

½ cup minced bacon

1. For grilled pizza, start a charcoal or wood fire or preheat a gas grill to the maximum. Roll or lightly press each dough ball into a flat round, lightly flouring the work surface and the dough as necessary (do not use more flour than you need to). Let the rounds sit for a few minutes, then roll or pat out the dough, as thinly as you like, turning occasionally and sprinkling the top with flour as necessary.

   For baked pizza, preheat the oven to 500°F. Oil one or more baking sheets, then press each dough ball into a flat round directly on the oiled sheet(s). Pat out the dough, as thinly as you like, oiling your hands if necessary. Or, if you have a baking stone, put it in the oven while preheating, then roll or pat out the dough as for grilled pizza, putting it on a peel to transfer it to the oven.

2. To grill the pizza, slide it directly onto the grill. Cook until brown grill marks appear, 3 to 5 minutes, depending on your grill heat. Turn with a spatula or tongs, then top with the arugula, corn, and bacon. Cover the grill and cook until the bottom is crisp and brown and the bacon cooked through.

To bake the pizza, top with the arugula, corn, and bacon, slide the baking sheet into the oven (or the pizza itself onto the stone), and bake for about 15 minutes, or until nicely browned.

Wine: Chianti or another rough red is usually best.

Serving: Roasted Red Peppers (Vegetables, page 58), Simple Green Salad (Vegetables, page 10), and/or Tomato Salad with Basil (Vegetables, page 20)

Pasta

Linguine with Fresh Herbs

All winter I dream of the time when there are so many fresh herbs that it seems imperative to use them at almost every meal. One of my favorite ways to take advantage of this abundance is to mix large quantities of herbs with pasta and a simple base of olive oil and garlic. In winter, a dish like this would not only seem exotic but would also cost a small fortune. In summer, however, it is an inexpensive no-brainer.

Makes: 4 to 6 servings

Time: 10 minutes

¼ cup extra virgin olive oil, or more to taste

1 teaspoon minced garlic

1 cup or more mixed fresh herbs, like parsley, dill, chervil, basil, tarragon, thyme, oregano, marjoram, or mint, woody or thick stems discarded

1 tablespoon unsalted butter (optional)

1 pound linguine or other long pasta

Salt and freshly ground black pepper

1. Bring a large pot of water to a boil. Combine the olive oil and garlic in a small saucepan over medium-low heat. Cook gently, just until the garlic begins to color, then remove from the heat. Meanwhile, wash and mince the herbs. Put them in a bowl large enough to hold the pasta. Cut the butter into bits if you're using it and add it to the bowl.

2. Salt the water and cook the pasta until tender but not mushy. Reserve ½ cup of the pasta-cooking water, then drain the pasta and toss with the herbs and reserved olive oil–garlic mixture. Add a little more olive oil or some of the pasta water if you did not use butter and the mixture seems dry. Season with salt and pepper and serve.

Wine: Crisp, dry white, like Orvieto, Pinot Grigio, or even Frascati

Serving: Salad (Grilled Bread Salad, page 78, would be perfect) or any vegetable would round out the meal.

Linguine with Tomato-Anchovy Sauce

Few things are simpler than tomato sauce over pasta, but as an unending diet it can become tiresome. Here it's completely jazzed by the addition of a hefty amount of garlic and a few anchovies.

Makes: 3 main-course to 6 first-course servings

Time: 30 minutes

---

2 tablespoons extra virgin olive oil

1 teaspoon minced garlic

4 to 6 anchovy fillets, with some of their oil

One 28-ounce can tomatoes, crushed or chopped and drained of their juice

1 pound linguine

Salt and freshly ground black pepper

1. Bring a large pot of water to a boil. Pour the oil into a deep skillet, turn the heat to medium, and heat for a minute. Add the garlic and the anchovies. When the garlic sizzles and the anchovies break up, add the tomatoes.

2. Turn the heat to medium-high and bring to a boil. Cook, stirring occasionally, until the mixture becomes saucy, about 15 minutes.

3. Salt the pasta water and cook the pasta until tender but not mushy. Season the sauce with salt and pepper to taste. Drain the pasta, toss it with the sauce, and serve.

Wine: Chianti or any spirited red

Serving: 60-Minute Bread (page 72) or good store-bought bread

Pasta with Parsley Sauce

Parsley is the most reliable and underrated herb in the western culinary world. Here, it is cooked like a vegetable—like spinach, really—to create a delicious, fresh-tasting pasta sauce, one that provides blessed relief in the winter and can become a staple in the summer.

Makes: 4 servings

Time: 20 to 30 minutes

2 tablespoons unsalted butter or extra virgin olive oil

¼ cup minced shallot or onion

2 or 3 bunches parsley (about 1 pound), stemmed, washed, and dried

1 cup heavy cream or half-and-half

1 pound cut pasta, such as ziti or penne

Salt and freshly ground black pepper

Freshly grated Parmigiano-Reggiano cheese

1. Bring a large pot of water to a boil for the pasta. Put the butter or oil in a deep skillet and turn the heat to medium. When the butter melts or the oil is hot, add the shallot or onion and cook, stirring occasionally, until softened, 3 to 5 minutes. Add the parsley and cook, stirring, for about a minute. Add the cream and turn the heat to low.

2. Salt the boiling water and cook the pasta until tender but not mushy. Season the parsley mixture with salt and pepper. Drain the pasta, toss it with the parsley mixture and some grated cheese, and serve.

Wine: Good Chardonnay or white Burgundy, preferably (real) Chablis

Serving: 60-Minute Bread (page 72) or good store-bought bread

Spaghetti with Fresh Tomato Sauce

This dish has a thick creaminess that you can never duplicate with canned tomatoes, no matter how good they are. So the season when you can make it—when there are good, ripe tomatoes in the market—is fairly short; where I live, just two or at the most three months a year.

There is an ideal instant for serving this sauce: When the tomatoes soften and all of their juices are in the skillet, the sauce suddenly begins to thicken. At that moment, it is at its peak; another minute or two later, many of the juices will have evaporated and, although the essence of the sauce is equally intense, it won't coat the pasta as well. If this happens, just add a little fresh olive oil or butter to the finished dish.

Makes: 4 to 6 servings

Time: 20 minutes

---

3 tablespoons unsalted butter or extra virgin olive oil

1½ to 2 pounds fresh tomatoes (preferably plum), cored and roughly chopped

1 pound spaghetti, linguine, or other long pasta

½ cup freshly grated Parmigiano-Reggiano cheese

Salt and freshly ground black pepper

1. Bring a large pot of water to a boil and salt it. Put the butter or oil in an 8- or 10-inch skillet over medium heat. When the butter melts or the oil is hot, add the tomatoes and turn the heat to high.

2. Cook, stirring occasionally, until the tomatoes begin to juice up, then turn the heat to low and cook, stirring occasionally, until the sauce thickens.

3. Cook the pasta until tender but not mushy. Drain and toss with the tomatoes and cheese. Season with salt and pepper to taste, toss again, and serve immediately.

Wine: A wide range of wines will work here, but I prefer good whites; Pinot Blanc is nice, or a good Chardonnay.

Serving: This is a good starter, followed by grilled meat, fish, and/or vegetables. Or you can serve bigger portions with a salad and bread.

Spaghetti with Zucchini

This dish, which has zucchini as its focus, is simply amazing when made in midsummer with tender, crisp squash, but it isn't half-bad even when made in midwinter with a limp vegetable that's traveled halfway around the world to get to your table. Either way, it is an unusual use for zucchini, which here substitutes for meat in a kind of vegetarian spaghetti carbonara, the rich pasta dish featuring eggs, bacon, and Parmesan. Made with zucchini instead of bacon, obviously, the dish becomes a little less fat-laden, but is still delicious.

Makes: 4 to 6 servings

Time: 30 minutes

3 tablespoons extra virgin olive oil

3 to 4 small zucchini (about 1 pound), washed, trimmed, and cut into slices ⅛ to ¼ inch thick

Salt and freshly ground black pepper

2 eggs

1 cup freshly grated Parmigiano-Reggiano cheese

1 pound spaghetti, linguine, or other long pasta

½ cup roughly chopped fresh mint, parsley, or basil

1. Bring a large pot of water to a boil and salt it. Place the olive oil in a 10- or 12-inch skillet over medium-high heat. A minute later, add the zucchini; cook, stirring only occasionally, until very tender and lightly browned, 10 to 15 minutes. Season with a little salt and a lot of pepper.

2. Meanwhile, beat the eggs and ½ cup of the Parmesan together. Add the pasta to the boiling water and cook until tender but not mushy. When it is done, drain and combine immediately with the egg-cheese mixture, tossing until the egg appears cooked. Stir in the zucchini, then taste and add more salt and pepper if necessary.

3. Toss in the herb and serve immediately, passing the remaining Parmesan at the table.

Wine: A good, rich Chardonnay

Serving: Bread and salad will do it.

Ziti with Butter, Sage, and Parmesan

The flour-enriched water in which pasta has cooked is never going to be an essential component of fine cooking, and it seldom appears in recipes. Yet from its origins as a cost-free, effortless substitute for stock, olive oil, butter, cream, or other occasionally scarce or even precious ingredients, pasta-cooking water has become a convenient and zero-calorie addition to simple sauces.

When you compare a lightly creamy sauce like the one in this recipe to the highly flavorful and ever-popular Alfredo sauce of butter, cream, eggs, and cheese, the latter seems relatively heavy. Substituting water for much of the butter and all of the cream and eggs produces a sauce with a perfect balance of weight and flavor. The water lends a quality not unlike that produced by tomatoes, as opposed to the slickness contributed by straight fat.

Makes: 4 to 6 servings

Time: 30 minutes

1 pound ziti, penne, or other cut pasta

2 tablespoons unsalted butter

30 fresh sage leaves

About 1 cup freshly grated Parmigiano-Reggiano cheese, plus more for serving

Salt and freshly ground black pepper

1. Bring a large pot of water to a boil and salt it. Cook the pasta until it is tender, but a little short of the point at which you want to eat it.

2. Meanwhile, put the butter in a skillet or saucepan large enough to hold the cooked pasta; turn the heat to medium and add the sage. Cook until the butter turns nut-brown and the sage shrivels, then turn the heat down to a minimum.

3. When the pasta is just about done, scoop out a cupful of the cooking water. Drain the pasta, immediately add it to the butter-sage mixture, and raise the heat to medium. Add ½ cup of the water and stir; the mixture will be loose and a little soupy. Cook for about 30 seconds, or until some of the water is absorbed and the pasta is perfectly done.

4. Stir in the cheese; the sauce will become creamy. Thin it with a little more pasta water if necessary, season liberally with salt and pepper to taste, and serve immediately, passing more cheese at the table if you like.

Wine: Almost any white, from a light one to a fine Chardonnay

Serving: This is best as a starter, not a main course, but it's still pretty rich. I would stick with a light fish preparation to follow—try Salmon and Tomatoes Cooked in foil (Meat, Fish & Poultry, page 10) for example—or perhaps a big salad.

Ziti with Chestnuts and Mushrooms

Chestnuts and dried mushrooms have a wonderful affinity for one another. Their unusual flavors and textures seem distantly related; they are both meaty and complex, chewy but neither tough nor crunchy. With shallots and plenty of black pepper for bite, the combination makes a great pasta sauce.

Although it may take thirty seconds to a minute to process a single chestnut, if you need only a dozen or so for a dish, the work amounts to about ten minutes. And in a creation like the one here, the time is well worth the effort.

Makes: 4 to 6 servings

Time: 30 minutes

---

15 chestnuts

1 ounce dried mushrooms—porcini, shiitakes, black trumpets, morels, or an assortment

3 tablespoons unsalted butter or extra virgin olive oil

½ cup peeled and sliced shallots

Salt and freshly ground black pepper

1 pound ziti or other cut pasta

1. Cut a ring around each chestnut, then place them in boiling water to cover and cook for 3 minutes. Remove them from the water, a few at a time, and peel while still hot. Meanwhile, soak the mushrooms in about 1½ cups very hot water.

2. Bring a large pot of water to a boil and salt it. Place half the butter or oil in a skillet, turn the heat to medium-high, and, a minute later, add the shallots. Sprinkle lightly with salt to taste and cook, stirring, until softened, 3 to 5 minutes. Chop the chestnuts into ½- to ¼-inch chunks, then measure about 1 cup. Add them to the skillet, along with a little more salt.

3. Cook, stirring occasionally, until the chestnuts deepen in color, about 5 minutes. Remove the mushrooms from their soaking liquid; strain, reserving the liquid. Chop the mushrooms and add them to the skillet; cook, stirring, for a minute or two, then add the strained mushroom-soaking liquid. Turn the heat to low and season to taste with salt and lots of black pepper.

4. Meanwhile, cook the pasta until tender but not mushy. If the sauce is too thick, add a little of the pasta-cooking water to it when the pasta is nearly done. Stir in the remaining butter or oil, then drain the pasta and dress with the sauce. Serve immediately.

Wine: A rich dish that will stand up to a good red—nothing lighter than Zinfandel, and Cabernet would not be out of place.

Serving: This can serve as a main course, and you don't need a lot else with it—some steamed broccoli or a salad and some bread. If you want to do a little work, Beet Roesti with Rosemary (Vegetables, page 24), would be a rewarding choice.

Penne with Butternut Squash

This dish is a minimalist's take on the northern Italian autumn staple of tortelli filled with zucca, a pumpkin-like vegetable whose flesh, like that of butternut or acorn squash, is dense, orange, and somewhat sweet. The flavor and essential nature of that dish can be captured in a thirty-minute preparation that turns the classic inside out, using the squash as a sauce and sparing you the hours it would take to stuff the tortelli.

Makes: 8 servings

Time: 30 minutes

1 pound peeled and seeded butternut squash (about 1½ pounds whole squash)

2 tablespoons unsalted butter or extra virgin olive oil

Salt and freshly ground black pepper

1 pound penne or other cut pasta

⅛ teaspoon freshly grated nutmeg, or to taste

1 teaspoon sugar, optional

½ cup freshly grated Parmigiano-Reggiano cheese

1. Cut the squash into chunks and put it in a food processor. Pulse the machine on and off until the squash appears grated. Alternatively, grate or finely chop the squash by hand. Bring a large pot of salted water to a boil for the pasta.

2. Put the butter or oil into a large skillet over medium heat. A minute later, add the squash, salt and pepper to taste, and about ½ cup of water. Cook over medium heat, stirring occasionally. Add water, about ¼ cup at a time, as the mixture dries out, but be careful not to make it soupy. When the squash begins to disintegrate, after 10 or 15 minutes, begin cooking the pasta. While it cooks, season the squash with the nutmeg, sugar if desired, and additional salt and pepper if needed.

3. When the pasta is tender, scoop out about ½ cup of the cooking liquid and reserve it, then drain the pasta. Toss the pasta in the skillet with the squash, adding the reserved pasta-cooking water if the mixture seems dry. Taste and add more of any seasonings you like, then toss with the Parmigiano-Reggiano and serve.

Wine: Light red, like Chianti or Beaujolais

Serving: Best as a starter, followed by roast poultry or some other hearty, simple main course (like Pot Roast with Cranberries in Meat, Fish & Poultry, page 66)

Pasta with Anchovies and Arugula

A quick way to add great flavor to many simple dinner dishes is already sitting in your pantry or cupboard: It's a can of anchovies. Anchovies are among the original convenience foods and contribute an intense shot of complex brininess that is more like Parmigiano-Reggiano than like canned tuna. Use them, along with garlic, as the base for a bold tomato sauce, or combine them, as I do here, with greens, garlic, oil, and chiles for a white sauce that packs a punch.

Makes: 3 main-course to 6 first-course servings

Time: 30 minutes

¼ cup extra virgin olive oil

4 large garlic cloves, peeled and slivered

8 anchovy fillets, or more to taste, with some of their oil

2 cups trimmed arugula, washed, dried, and chopped

1 pound linguine or other long pasta

Salt and freshly ground black pepper

½ teaspoon crushed red pepper flakes, or more to taste

1. Bring a large pot of water to a boil for the pasta. Pour 2 tablespoons of the oil into a deep skillet, turn the heat to medium, and heat for a minute. Add the garlic and anchovies. When the garlic sizzles and the anchovies break up, turn the heat to the minimum.

2. Salt the boiling water and cook the pasta until tender but not mushy. Reserve 1 cup of the cooking liquid and drain. Add the pasta and the arugula to the skillet, along with enough of the reserved cooking water to make a sauce; turn the heat to medium and stir for a minute. Add salt and pepper to taste, plus a pinch or more of the red pepper flakes.

3. Turn into a bowl, toss with the remaining 2 tablespoons oil, and serve.

Wine: White and very crisp, like Muscadet or Pinot Grigio; inexpensive Chardonnay would also be good.

Serving: Roasted Red Peppers (Vegetables, page 58), 60-Minute Bread (page 72) or good store-bought bread

Pasta with Cauliflower

Pasta with stewed vegetables—I most often choose cauliflower, but there are many other options—is the one-pot meal I turn to most often when I'm desperate to get something quick, healthy, and filling on the table. It begins with poaching cauliflower, then uses the same water to cook the pasta. The cauliflower and pasta ultimately finish cooking in a mix of extra virgin olive oil, garlic, bread crumbs, and some of the reserved cooking water. The fundamental procedures are easy, and build a wonderfully flavorful dish with just a few ingredients.

Makes: 3 main-course to 6 first-course servings

Time: 40 minutes

1 head cauliflower (about 1 pound)

¼ cup extra virgin olive oil

1 tablespoon minced garlic

1 cup coarse bread crumbs

1 pound penne, ziti, or other cut pasta

Salt and freshly ground black pepper

1. Bring a large pot of water to a boil. Trim the cauliflower and divide it into florets. Salt the water, add the cauliflower, and cook until the cauliflower is tender but not mushy. Remove the cauliflower with a slotted spoon and set it aside; when it is cool enough to handle, chop it roughly into small pieces.

2. Combine the oil and garlic in a large, deep skillet over medium-low heat and cook, stirring occasionally, until the garlic is golden, about 5 minutes. Meanwhile, cook the pasta in the same water that you used for the cauliflower.

3. When the garlic is golden, add the cauliflower and bread crumbs to the skillet and turn the heat to medium. Cook, stirring occasionally. When the pasta is just about done—it should be 2 or 3 minutes shy of being the way you like it—drain it, reserving about a cup of the cooking liquid.

4. Add the pasta to the skillet with the cauliflower and toss with a large spoon until well combined. Add salt and pepper to taste, along with some of the pasta water to keep the mixture from drying out. When the mixture is hot and the pasta tender and nicely glazed, serve.

Wine: Chianti, Beaujolais, or another light red

Serving: Simple Green Salad (Vegetables, page 10)

Pasta with Clams and Tomatoes

Every time I think I have come up with the ultimate pasta and clam dish, someone shows me a better one. This is a technique I learned in Liguria—the Italian Riviera—in which all of the clam liquid is used as part of the sauce, but without much effort. The result is delicious pasta in a rich, thick sauce—along with a pile of clams.

Makes: 3 main-course to 6 first-course servings

Time: 30 to 40 minutes

¼ cup extra virgin olive oil

36 to 48 littleneck clams, well washed

1 tablespoon minced garlic

1 pound linguine or other long pasta

2 or 3 plum tomatoes, cored and chopped

Salt and freshly ground black pepper

Chopped fresh parsley

1. Bring a large pot of water to a boil for the pasta. Pour 2 tablespoons of the oil into a large, deep skillet, turn the heat to high, and heat for a minute. Add the clams, reduce the heat to medium-high, give the pan a shake, and cover. Continue to cook the clams, shaking the pan occasionally, until they begin to open, about 5 minutes. Add the garlic and cook until most of the clams are open.

2. Salt the boiling water and cook the pasta. When it is nearly tender, remove a cup of the cooking water and drain. When the clams are ready, add the pasta and the tomatoes to the skillet and cook, tossing frequently, until the pasta is tender and hot; add some of the pasta-cooking water if the mixture is too dry.

3. Add the remaining 2 tablespoons oil, add salt and pepper to taste, garnish with the parsley, and serve.

Wine: Pinot Grigio, Orvieto, Vernaccia, or another crisp Italian white

Serving: 60-Minute Bread (page 72) or good store-bought bread

Pasta with Gorgonzola and Arugula

This pasta boasts just a couple of main ingredients and a supporting cast of two staples.

Makes: 8 servings

Time: 30 minutes

4 tablespoons (½ stick) unsalted butter

½ pound ripe Gorgonzola

2 pounds cut pasta, like ziti or farfalle

12 ounces arugula

Salt and freshly ground black pepper

1. Bring a large pot of water to a boil for the pasta. Meanwhile, melt the butter over low heat in a small saucepan; add the Gorgonzola and cook, stirring frequently, until the cheese melts. Keep warm while you cook the pasta.

2. Tear the arugula into bits—the pieces should not be too small. Salt the boiling water and cook the pasta until tender but not mushy. Remove and reserve a little of the cooking water, then drain the pasta and toss it with the arugula and the cheese mixture, adding a bit of the cooking water if the mixture seems dry.

3. Taste and adjust the seasoning—use plenty of black pepper—and serve.

Wine: A dry Chardonnay

Serving: Grilled White-and-Sweet Potato Salad (Vegetables, page 62)

Pasta with Walnuts

You might think of this as winter pesto, with a higher percentage of walnuts and the always-available parsley filling in for summer's basil.

Makes: 8 servings

Time: 20 to 30 minutes

2 cups walnuts or pecan halves

1 cup loosely packed fresh parsley or basil leaves

2 garlic cloves

1 cup extra virgin olive oil, plus more if needed

Salt and freshly ground black pepper

2 pounds linguine, spaghetti, or other long pasta

1. Bring a large pot of water to a boil and salt it. Meanwhile, combine the nuts, parsley or basil, and garlic in a small food processor and turn the machine on. With the machine running, add the oil gradually, using just enough so that the mixture forms a creamy paste. Season to taste with salt and pepper.

2. Cook the pasta, stirring occasionally, until tender but not mushy. When it is ready, drain it—reserve some of the cooking water—and toss with the sauce; if the mixture appears too thick, thin with a little of the pasta cooking water (or more olive oil). Serve.

Wine: A fruity red is in order: perhaps a Côtes du Rhône blend, or a Chianti Classico.

Serving: Canapés with Piquillo Peppers and Anchovies (Small Plates & Soups, page 17), and Osso Buco (Meat, Fish & Poultry, page 70)

Pasta alla Gricia

There is an important and splendid group of pasta recipes associated with Rome and the area around it; all the variations begin with bits of cured meat cooked until crisp. Around these delightfully crispy bits—and, of course, their rendered fat—are built a number of different sauces of increasing complexity. The first contains no more than meat and grated cheese and is called pasta alla gricia; the second, in which eggs are added, is the well-known pasta (usually spaghetti) carbonara, one of the first authentic nontomato pasta dishes to become popular in the United States, about thirty years ago; and the third is pasta all' Amatriciana, which adds the sweetness of cooked onions and the acidity of tomatoes.

Makes: 3 main-course to 6 first-course servings

Time: 30 minutes

2 tablespoons extra virgin olive oil

½ cup minced guanciale, pancetta, or bacon (about ¼ pound)

1 pound linguine or other long pasta

½ cup grated Pecorino Romano, or more to taste

Freshly ground black pepper

1. Bring a large pot of water to a boil for the pasta. In a medium saucepan, combine the oil and meat and turn the heat to medium. Cook, stirring occasionally, until the meat is nicely browned, about 10 minutes. Turn off the heat.

2. Salt the boiling water and cook the pasta until tender but not mushy. Before draining the pasta, remove about a cup of the cooking water and reserve it.

3. Toss the drained pasta with the meat and its juices; stir in the cheese. If the mixture is dry, add a little of the pasta cooking water (or a little olive oil). Toss in lots of black pepper and serve.

Wine: Crisp white, like Pinot Grigio or even Frascati

Serving: 60-Minute Bread (page 72) or good store-bought bread; Simple Green Salad (Vegetables, page 10)

Pasta with Green Beans, Potatoes, and Pesto

Pesto has become a staple, especially in late summer when basil is at its best. But pasta with pesto does have its limits; it's simply not substantial enough to serve as a main course. The Genoese, originators of pesto, figured this out centuries ago when they created trenette with pesto. Trenette is a pasta almost identical to linguine, and trenette with pesto (trenette is always served with pesto) often contains chunks of potatoes and green beans, which make it more complex, more filling, and more interesting than plain pasta with pesto. Recreating this classic dish is straightforward and easy.

Makes: 3 main-course to 6 first-course servings

Time: 30 minutes

---

2 cups fresh basil leaves

2 garlic cloves, peeled

Salt

½ cup grated Pecorino Romano or other hard sheep's-milk cheese or Parmigiano-Reggiano

½ cup extra virgin olive oil, or more to taste

2 tablespoons pine nuts

2 medium potatoes (about ½ pound), peeled and cut into ½-inch cubes

1 pound trenette or linguine

½ pound green beans, trimmed and cut into 1-inch lengths

1. Bring a large pot of water to a boil for the potatoes and pasta. Combine the basil, garlic, salt to taste, and cheese in a blender or food processor; pulse until roughly chopped. Add ½ cup oil in a steady stream and continue to blend until the mixture is fairly creamy, adding a little more oil or some water if necessary. Add the pine nuts and pulse a few times to chop them into the sauce.

2. Salt the boiling water. Add the potatoes and stir; cook for 3 minutes, then add the pasta and cook as usual, stirring frequently, about 10 minutes. When the pasta is about half done—the strands will bend but are not yet tender—add the green beans.

3. When the pasta is done, the potatoes and beans should be tender. Drain the pasta and vegetables, toss with pesto and more salt or olive oil, if you like, and serve.

Wine: Beaujolais, Chianti, or another light, fruity red

Serving: Assuming it's summer, Raw Beet Salad (Vegetables, page 27) or Simple Green Salad (Vegetables, page 10)

Pasta with Red Wine Sauce

Finishing pasta by cooking it for the final minute or two in stock is not all that uncommon. But simmering it in flavorful liquid for nearly all of its cooking time—almost as you would a risotto—is highly unusual. And when that liquid is red wine, the pasta is, well, unique. This dish was created by Alessandro Giuntoli, a Tuscan chef. It is in fact much better suited to home than restaurant cooking, because it must be prepared entirely at the last minute. It's simple enough, and there are aspects of it that are quite splendid: The pasta takes on a fruity acidity—smoothed by the last-minute addition of butter—and a beautiful mahogany glaze that's like nothing you've ever seen.

Makes: About 4 servings

Time: 30 minutes

½ cup extra virgin olive oil

1 tablespoon minced garlic

1 teaspoon crushed red pepper flakes, or to taste

1 pound spaghetti

Salt and freshly ground black pepper

1 bottle red wine, such as Chianti

1 tablespoon unsalted butter

1. Bring a large pot of water to a boil and salt it. Place the oil, garlic, and red pepper in a large, deep skillet.

2. When the water boils, add the pasta; turn the heat under the skillet to high. Cook the pasta as usual, stirring. As soon as the garlic begins to brown, sprinkle it with salt and pepper to taste and add three-fourths of the bottle of wine (a little more than 2 cups); bring to a boil and maintain it there.

3. When the pasta begins to bend—after less than 5 minutes of cooking—drain it and add it to the wine mixture. Cook, stirring occasionally, adding wine a little at a time if the mixture threatens to dry out completely.

4. Taste the pasta frequently. When it is done—tender but with a little bite—stir in the butter and turn off the heat. When the butter glazes the pasta, serve it immediately.

Wine: A challenge; you can choose the same kind of wine that you use in the dish, but you're not going to want a lot of it. I'd drink water and save wine for the second course.

Serving: This is a true starter, not a main course; follow it with something gutsy, like grilled meat or fish, or something grand like Crisp Roasted Rack of Lamb (Meat, Fish & Poultry, page 72).

Pasta with Fast Sausage Ragù

True ragù is a magnificent pasta sauce, a slow-simmered blend of meat, tomatoes, and milk. The real thing takes hours, for the meat must become tender and contribute its silkiness to the sauce, the tomatoes must dissolve, and the milk must pull the whole thing together. But a reasonable approximation of ragù can be produced using ground beef or pork or, even better, prepared Italian sausage.

Makes: 8 servings

Time: 30 minutes

1 tablespoon extra virgin olive oil

1 large onion, chopped

1 pound Italian sausage, removed from casing if necessary

2 cups milk, plus more if necessary

½ cup tomato paste

Salt and freshly ground black pepper

Chicken stock (optional)

2 pounds long pasta (fresh, if available)

About 2 cups freshly grated Parmesan

1. Set a large pot of water to boil for the pasta. Put the oil in a 10-inch skillet and turn the heat to medium; a minute later add the onion. Cook, stirring occasionally, until it softens, about 5 minutes. Add the sausage in bits and turn the heat to medium-high; cook, stirring infrequently, until the sausage is nicely browned, 5 to 10 minutes.

2. Add the milk and tomato paste, along with some salt and pepper; stir to blend and simmer for about 5 minutes, or until thick but not dry. Keep it warm if necessary and, if it becomes too thick, add a little more milk, water, or chicken stock.

3. Meanwhile, salt the water and cook the pasta. When the pasta is tender but not mushy, drain it. Toss with the sauce and about half the Parmesan. Taste and adjust the seasoning; serve, passing the remaining Parmesan at the table.

Wine: Chianti or any other fruity but gutsy red, like Zinfandel or a Côtes du Rhône

Serving: Chicken with Pancetta and Balsamic Vinegar (Meat, Fish & Poultry, page 48) and Porcini-Scented "Wild" Mushroom Sauté (Vegetables, page 76)

Pasta with Dark Red Duck Sauce

Every visitor to Tuscany comes away with a love of this nearly brown sauce, which can be made with duck or similar quantities of rabbit, beef, or pork.

Makes: 8 servings

Time: 2 hours or more, largely unattended

4 duck legs

1 large onion, chopped

3 cups dry red wine

One 28-ounce can plum tomatoes, drained and roughly chopped

Salt and freshly ground black pepper

1 pound cut pasta, such as penne

Freshly grated Pecorino Romano or Parmesan cheese

1. Trim the visible fat from the duck legs, then lay them, skin side down, in a large skillet. Turn the heat to medium and, when the duck begins to sizzle, turn the heat to low and cover. Cook undisturbed for about an hour (check once to make sure the legs aren't burning and adjust the heat if necessary), by which time the skin should be golden brown. Turn, cover again, and cook until the duck is very tender, at least 30 minutes more.

2. Remove the duck and set aside; remove most but not all of the fat. Add the onion to the skillet and turn the heat to medium-high. Cook, stirring occasionally, until the onion is softened, about 5 minutes. Set a large pot of water to boil for the pasta and salt it.

3. Add the wine to the onion and raise the heat to high; cook until the liquid is reduced by about half, then add the tomatoes along with some salt and pepper and cook over medium-high heat, stirring occasionally, until the mixture is saucy, about 15 minutes. Taste and adjust the seasoning.

4. Meanwhile, shred the duck from the bone and add it to the sauce as it cooks. A few minutes after adding the tomatoes, cook the pasta. When it is tender but not mushy, drain the pasta and serve it with the sauce, along with the cheese.

Wine: Dark and red: Something made with the Nebbiolo grape (like Barolo or Barbaresco) would be ideal. For cooking, use something less expensive, like a fairly standard Cabernet or Zinfandel.

Serving: Cauliflower with Garlic and Anchovy (Vegetables, page 86)

Pasta with Meaty Bones

A basic tomato sauce is (or at least should be) a part of every cook's repertoire, since it's among the most fundamental dressings for pasta. Typically, you make this sauce by coloring a little garlic or onion in oil, then adding crushed tomatoes and cooking them over medium-high heat. When the mixture becomes "saucy," about twenty minutes later, it's done.

The variations on this theme are nearly infinite. One of my favorites is southern Italian in origin. It begins with bony meat (or meaty bones) and requires lengthy simmering.

Whatever you use, the idea remains constant: Meat is a supporting player, not the star, so an 8- to 12-ounce piece of veal shank, for example, provides enough meat, marrow, and gelatin to create a luxuriously rich sauce. Just cook until the meat falls off the bone, then chop it and return it to the sauce along with any marrow.

Makes: 4 to 6 servings

Time: At least 1 hour

---

2 tablespoons extra virgin olive oil

2 small dried hot red chiles (optional)

1 piece meaty veal shank, ½ to 1 pound

3 garlic cloves, peeled and roughly chopped

Salt and freshly ground black pepper

One 28-ounce can whole plum tomatoes, with juice

1 pound ziti, penne, or other cut pasta

½ cup or more roughly chopped fresh parsley or basil

1. Pour the olive oil into a saucepan over medium heat. After a minute, add the chiles, if using, and cook for about 30 seconds. Add the veal shank and raise the heat to medium-high; cook, turning as necessary, until the meat is nicely browned, 10 minutes or more. When the meat is just about done, add the garlic and salt and pepper to taste.

2. When the garlic has softened a bit, crush the tomatoes and add them along with their juice. Turn the heat to medium-low to maintain a steady simmer. If you are using a broad pot, cover it partially. Cook, stirring occasionally, until the meat is tender and just about falling off the bone, at least 1 hour.

3. Bring a large pot of water to a boil and salt it. Cook the pasta until tender but not mushy. Remove the veal shank, scoop out any marrow, chop the meat coarsely, and return the meat to the sauce (discard the bone). Remove and discard the chiles.

4. Drain and sauce the pasta; sprinkle it with the herb, toss, and serve.

Wine: Red and big: Barolo, Cabernet, or very good Zinfandel

Serving: You don't need anything else, but salad or a light vegetable dish (see Green Beans with Lemon, Vegetables, page 30) wouldn't hurt. Don't fuss, though.

Stir-Fried Coconut Noodles

Rice noodles have no equivalent in European cooking. Made from rice powder and almost always sold dried, they are nearly as fast-cooking as fresh wheat noodles. Regardless of their name (rice stick, rice vermicelli, oriental-style noodle, and so on), rice noodles are easily recognized by their gray-white, translucent appearance, and by the fact that because of their somewhat irregular shapes, they are never packed in as orderly a fashion as wheat noodles. (They are quite long and are packaged folded up over themselves.) Two thicknesses are common: very thin and fettuccine-like; here you want the latter.

Makes: 4 servings

Time: 45 minutes

---

1 pound fettuccine-style rice noodles

3 tablespoons grapeseed, corn, or other light oil

1 pound minced or ground boneless pork or chicken

1 yellow or red bell pepper, stemmed, seeded, and minced

1 eggplant (about ½ pound), cut into ½-inch cubes

1 tablespoon minced garlic

One 12- to 14-ounce can (about 1½ cups) unsweetened coconut milk

Nam pla (fish sauce), soy sauce, or salt

Freshly ground black pepper

Minced cilantro

1. Soak the noodles in very hot water to cover until you're ready to add them to the stir-fry.

2. Meanwhile, pour 1 tablespoon of the oil into a large skillet or wok, turn the heat to high, and heat for a minute. Add the meat and cook, stirring occasionally, until it browns and loses its raw look, about 5 minutes. Remove with a slotted spoon and set aside.

3. Add another 1 tablespoon oil to the skillet, followed by the bell pepper and eggplant. Cook over medium-high heat, stirring occasionally, until the pepper and eggplant are browned and tender, about 10 minutes. Remove with a slotted spoon and combine with the meat.

4. Add the remaining 1 tablespoon oil, followed immediately by the garlic, and cook for about 30 seconds. Add the coconut milk. Cook over medium-high heat, stirring and scraping with a wooden spoon, for about a minute. Drain the noodles and add along with the meat and vegetables. Cook until the noodles absorb most of the coconut milk, about 3 minutes.

5. Season with nam pla, soy sauce, or salt to taste, then add plenty of black pepper. Garnish with cilantro and serve.

Wine: Beer, Pinot Blanc, not-too-sweet Gewürztraminer or Riesling

Serving: Herbed Green Salad with Soy Vinaigrette (Vegetables, page 12)

Rice Noodles with Basil

In a stir-fry like this, you can get away with simply soaking rice noodles, but I believe boiling the noodles for 30 seconds or so after soaking improves them a bit. Try it and see. Substitute soy sauce for the nam pla if you like. Thai basil, which looks different from regular basil, can be found at many Asian markets; it's fabulously fragrant.

Makes: 4 servings

Time: 40 minutes

¾ pound rice noodles (rice stick)

2 tablespoons peanut or vegetable oil

1 tablespoon minced garlic

1 teaspoon minced fresh hot chiles or crushed red pepper flakes, or to taste

1 teaspoon sugar

Salt and freshly ground black pepper

2 tablespoons nam pla (fish sauce) or soy sauce, or to taste

1 tablespoon fresh lime juice, or to taste

½ cup roughly chopped fresh Thai or other basil or mint

1. Soak the rice noodles in hot water to cover for 15 to 30 minutes, changing the water once or twice if possible to speed the softening. Meanwhile, bring a pot of water to a boil. When the noodles are soft, drain them, then immerse in the boiling water for about 30 seconds. Drain and rinse in cold water.

2. Heat the oil in a deep skillet, preferably nonstick, over medium-high heat. Add the garlic and chiles and cook for about 30 seconds, stirring. Raise the heat to high, then add the noodles and sugar and toss to blend. Season with salt and pepper to taste.

3. When the noodles are hot, add the nam pla and lime juice. Taste and adjust the seasoning as necessary, then stir in the basil or mint and serve.

Wine: Beer is the best choice.

Serving: Follow or serve with stir-fried vegetables or a meat- or fish-and-vegetable stir-fry. Chicken Curry with Coconut Milk (Meat, Fish & Poultry, page 38) would make a feast out of this.

Stir-Fried Noodles with Shrimp

Here's another use for rice noodles. This one is akin to the popular (in the U.S. at least) Thai restaurant dish known as pad Thai. There are a lot of ingredients here, but most of them keep well in your pantry, and substituting is easy.

Makes: 4 servings

Time: 30 to 40 minutes

6 dried black (shiitake) mushrooms (or use fresh shiitakes, trimmed of their stems and sliced)

12 ounces thin rice noodles (vermicelli or rice stick)

2 tablespoons peanut or grapeseed, corn, or other light oil

1 tablespoon slivered or minced garlic

12 ounces shrimp, peeled (deveined if you like) and cut into bite-size pieces

½ teaspoon Asian chile paste or crushed red pepper flakes, or to taste

2 eggs, lightly beaten

3 tablespoons soy sauce, or to taste

2 teaspoons sugar

Stock (or water or mushroom-soaking liquid) as needed

Salt (optional)

1 cup bean sprouts (optional)

½ cup washed, dried, and torn fresh basil leaves, preferably Thai basil (optional)

1. Put the dried mushrooms in a small bowl and cover them with boiling water (don't soak fresh mushrooms). Put the noodles in a large bowl and cover them with hot water. Prepare the other ingredients. When the mushrooms are soft, about 10 minutes later, drain, reserving their soaking liquid; trim and slice them.

2. Put the oil in a large nonstick skillet and turn the heat to high. Add the garlic and stir; add the shrimp and cook, stirring occasionally, for about a minute. Stir in the chile paste.

3. Drain the noodles and add to the skillet. Cook, stirring occasionally, for about a minute. Make a well in the center of the noodles and pour the eggs into this well. Scramble, gradually integrating the egg with the noodles; this will take less than a minute. Stir in the soy sauce and sugar. If the noodles are "clumpy," add about ½ cup of liquid to allow them to separate and become saucy (use more liquid if necessary, but do not make the mixture soupy). Add salt to taste, then stir in the bean sprouts and basil, if using, and the sliced mushrooms. Cook another 30 seconds, then serve.

Wine: Beer or not-too-dry Gewürztraminer or Riesling

Serving: Herbed Green Salad with Soy Vinaigrette (Vegetables, page 12)

Crisp Pan-Fried Noodle Cake

This recipe makes one noodle cake, which can be stretched to serve eight; but I recommend making two. You can prepare everything in one bowl, but cook the two cakes separately.

Makes: 1 cake

Time: 30 minutes

12 ounces fresh egg noodles, or 8 ounces dried pasta

¼ cup minced scallions

1 tablespoon soy sauce

¼ cup peanut (preferred) or other oil, plus more if needed

1. Cook the noodles in boiling salted water until tender but not mushy. Drain, then rinse in cold water for a minute or two. Toss with the scallions, soy sauce, and 1 tablespoon of the oil.

2. Pour the remaining oil into a heavy medium to large skillet, preferably nonstick; turn the heat to medium-high. When the oil is hot, add the noodle mix, spreading it out evenly and pressing it down.

3. Cook 2 minutes, then turn the heat to medium-low. Continue to cook until the cake holds together and is nicely browned on the bottom. Turn carefully (the easiest way to do this is to slide the cake out onto a plate, cover it with another plate, invert the plates, and slide the cake back into the skillet, browned side up), adding a little more oil if necessary.

4. Cook on the other side until brown and serve.

Wine: Beer would be preferable, but if you insist on wine, try a Gewürztraminer. Champagne is always suitable, too.

Serving: Slow-Cooked Ribs with Black Beans (Meat, Fish & Poultry, page 86) and Herbed Green Salad with Nut Vinaigrette (Vegetables, page 11)

Fresh Chinese Noodles with Brown Sauce

You can find fresh Chinese- (and Japanese-) style noodles in most supermarkets these days. They're a great convenience food, and for some reason seem more successful than prepackaged "fresh" Italian noodles. Here, they're briefly cooked and then combined with a stir-fried mixture of pork, vegetables, and Chinese sauces; it's very much a Chinese restaurant dish.

Makes: 4 servings

Time: 20 to 30 minutes

½ to 1 pound ground pork

1 cup minced scallions

1 tablespoon peeled and minced fresh ginger

1 tablespoon minced garlic

1 cup chicken stock or water

2 tablespoons ground bean sauce

2 tablespoon hoisin sauce

1 tablespoon soy sauce

1 pound fresh egg or wheat noodles (see headnote)

1 tablespoon toasted sesame oil

1. Bring a large pot of water to a boil for the noodles. Meanwhile, put a large skillet over medium-high heat. Add the pork, crumbling it to bits as you add it and stirring to break up any clumps. Add ½ cup of the scallions, along with the ginger and garlic, and stir. Add the stock or water; stir in the bean, hoisin, and soy sauces and cook, stirring occasionally, until thick, about 5 minutes. Reduce the heat and keep warm.

2. Cook the noodles, stirring, until tender, 3 to 5 minutes. Drain and dress with the sauce. Garnish with the remaining ½ cup scallions, drizzle the sesame oil over all, and serve.

Wine: Beer or not-too-dry Gewürztraminer or Riesling

Serving: Herbed Green Salad with Soy Vinaigrette (Vegetables, page 12) and steamed vegetables

Cold Noodles with Sesame Sauce

One of the best make-in-advance side dishes, and a plus at almost any buffet. Not bad as a main course, either, especially if you shred some cooked chicken into it.

Makes: 4 to 6 servings

Time: About 40 minutes

---

12 ounces fresh Chinese egg noodles or dried pasta

2 tablespoons toasted sesame oil

¼ cup sesame paste (tahini) or natural peanut butter

1 tablespoon sugar

¼ cup soy sauce

1 tablespoon rice or wine vinegar

Tabasco or other hot sauce

Salt and freshly ground black pepper

At least ½ cup minced scallions

1. Bring a large pot of salted water to a boil. Cook the noodles until they are tender but not mushy. Drain, then rinse in cold water for a minute or two. Toss with 1 tablespoon of the oil and refrigerate for up to 2 hours, or proceed with the recipe.

2. Beat together the tahini, sugar, soy sauce, vinegar, and remaining 1 tablespoon oil. Add a little hot sauce and salt and pepper; taste and adjust the seasoning as necessary. Thin the sauce with hot water, so that it is about the consistency of heavy cream.

3. Toss together the noodles and the sauce, and add more of any seasoning if necessary. Garnish with the scallions and serve.

Wine: Beer or not-too-dry Gewürztraminer or Riesling

Serving: Herbed Green Salad with Soy Vinaigrette (Vegetables, page 12)

Grains

"Risotto" with Coconut Milk and Seafood

The creaminess that is the ideal in a finished risotto is not always easy to achieve. And the peak of creaminess does not necessarily coincide with the rice being cooked to the correct degree (which is, most believe, just a shade shy of complete tenderness). A load of butter helps, but most home cooks are reluctant to add this. Coconut milk, however, adds not only distinctive flavor, depth, and a touch of sweetness to a risotto, it practically guarantees a creamy result.

Makes: 8 servings

Time: 40 minutes

---

2 tablespoons vegetable oil

2 cups short-grain rice, such as Arborio

1½ cups dry white wine

Two 14-ounce cans coconut milk

1 cup diced tomato (canned is fine; drain well), optional

1 pound peeled and diced shrimp

Salt

¼ teaspoon cayenne, or to taste

½ cup minced fresh basil, cilantro, or scallions (optional)

1. Put the oil in a 10-inch skillet, preferably nonstick, and turn the heat to medium-high. Add the rice and cook, stirring occasionally, until the rice glistens and sizzles, 2 to 3 minutes. Put a small pot of water (2 or 3 cups) on the stove to heat up.

2. Add the wine and let it boil away, stirring once or twice, until the mixture is just about dry. Add 1 cup of the hot water and repeat, stirring frequently. Add half the coconut milk and, once again, cook, stirring frequently, until it is just about gone. Add the remaining coconut milk and repeat.

3. At this point the rice should be nearly tender; if it is not, repeat the process with another ½ cup hot water, or more if necessary. Stir in the tomato, if using, shrimp, salt to taste, and cayenne and cook until the mixture is creamy and the rice is tender but not mushy. (If the rice is still too crunchy for your taste, stir in another ½ cup hot water and cook, stirring, until the mixture is creamy again.) Garnish with basil, if you like, and serve.

Wine: A fruity one, like Gewürztraminer or Riesling

Serving: Herbed Green Salad with Soy Vinaigrette (Vegetables, page 12)

60-Minute Bread

Makes: 1 loaf

Time: 1 to 2 hours, largely unattended

---

3 cups all-purpose flour, plus more as needed

2 teaspoons instant yeast, such as SAF

2 teaspoons salt

1. Combine the flour, yeast, and salt in a bowl or food processor Add 1¼ cups warm water all at once, stirring with a wooden spoon or mixing with the machine on. Continue to mix for a minute or two longer by hand, about 30 seconds total with the food processor. Add more water by the tablespoon if necessary, until a ball forms.

2. Shape the dough into a flat round or long loaf. Place the dough on a baking sheet or a well-floured pizza peel. Let it rise in the warmest place in your kitchen, covered, while you preheat the oven to 425°F. (If you have time, let it rise for an hour or so.) If you have a baking stone, preheat in the oven.

3. Bake the bread on a sheet, or slide it onto a baking stone. Bake until done, 30 to 45 minutes.

Wine: Depends on main course

Serving: Makes a wonderful addition to complete most meals

Corn Bread

Corn bread is a quick bread—that is, risen with baking powder, not yeast—and the most useful one of all. Everyone loves it, too.

Makes: 6 servings

Time: 45 minutes

---

2 tablespoons unsalted butter or extra virgin olive oil

1½ cups cornmeal

½ cup flour

1½ teaspoons baking powder

1 teaspoon salt

2 tablespoons sugar

1 egg

1¼ cups buttermilk, milk, or yogurt

1. Preheat the oven to 375°F. Heat the fat in a medium nonstick or well-seasoned ovenproof skillet or in an 8-inch square baking pan over medium heat until good and hot, about 2 minutes, then turn off the heat.

2. Meanwhile, combine the dry ingredients in a bowl. Mix the egg into the buttermilk, then stir the liquid mixture into the dry ingredients, combining well; if it seems too dry, add another tablespoon or two of buttermilk. Pour the batter into the preheated fat, shake the pan once or twice, and put in the oven.

3. Bake for about 30 minutes, until the top is lightly browned and the sides have pulled away from the pan.

Wine: Depends on main course

Serving: Makes a wonderful addition to complete most meals

Spanish Tortilla

The Spanish tortilla has nothing in common with the Mexican tortilla except its name, which comes from the Latin *torta*—a round cake. In its most basic form, the Spanish tortilla is a potato-and-egg frittata, or omelet, which derives most of its flavor from olive oil. Although the ingredients are simple and minimal, when made correctly—and there is a straightforward but very definite series of techniques involved—this tortilla is wonderfully juicy. And because it is better at room temperature than hot, it can and in fact should be made in advance. (How much in advance is up to you. It can be fifteen minutes or a few hours.)

Makes: 3 to 6 servings

Time: About 40 minutes

1¼ pounds potatoes, 3 to 4 medium

1 medium onion

1 cup extra virgin olive oil

Salt and freshly ground black pepper

6 extra-large or jumbo eggs

1. Peel and thinly slice the potatoes and onion; it's easiest if you use a mandolin for slicing. Meanwhile, heat the oil in an 8- or 10-inch skillet over medium heat. After 3 to 4 minutes, drop in a slice of potato. When tiny bubbles appear around the edges of the potato, the oil is ready. Add all of the potatoes and onion along with a good pinch of salt and a liberal sprinkling of pepper. Gently turn the potato mixture in the oil with a wooden spoon, and adjust the heat so that the oil bubbles lazily.

2. Cook, turning the potatoes gently every few minutes and adjusting the heat so they do not brown, until they are tender when pierced with the point of a small knife. If the potatoes begin to break, they are overdone—stop the cooking immediately. As the potatoes cook, beat the eggs with some salt and pepper in a large bowl.

3. Drain the potatoes in a colander, reserving the oil. Heat an 8- or 10-inch nonstick skillet over medium heat for a minute and add 2 tablespoons of the reserved oil. Gently mix the warm potatoes with the eggs and add them to the skillet. As soon as the edges firm up— this will take only a minute or so—reduce the heat to medium-low. Cook 5 minutes.

4. Insert a rubber spatula all around the edges of the cake to make sure it will slide from the pan. Carefully slide it out—the top will still be quite runny—onto a plate. Cover with another plate and, holding the plates tightly, invert them. Add another tablespoon of oil to the skillet and use a rubber spatula to coax the cake back in. Cook another 5 minutes, then slide the cake from the skillet to a plate. (Alternatively, finish the cooking by putting the tortilla in a 350°F oven for about 10 minutes.) Serve warm (not hot) or at room temperature. Do not refrigerate.

Wine: Rioja or other soft, light red

Serving: This is most frequently served as a tapa— snack—in Spain, but it's a great starter or main course, depending on quantity. With bread and a salad, it makes a complete meal.

Persian Rice
with Potatoes

A perfect side dish for the lean fish. Skimp on the butter if you like, but the potatoes will not be as crisp or delicious. Better, I think, to switch to olive oil.

Makes: 8 servings

Time: About 2 hours, largely unattended

2 cups good long-grain rice, like basmati

4 to 6 tablespoons unsalted butter or extra virgin olive oil

1 pound russet or other all-purpose potatoes, peeled and thinly sliced

Salt and freshly ground black pepper

1. Bring a large pot of water to a boil and salt it; add the rice and cook, stirring occasionally, as you would pasta. When it is nearly done, drain it.

2. While the rice is cooking, heat 2 tablespoons of the butter over medium heat in a wide skillet or casserole, preferably nonstick. Arrange the potatoes in the butter and sprinkle with salt and pepper. When the rice is done, pour it over the potatoes and turn the heat to very low. Add 2 more tablespoons of butter and cover. Cook over the lowest possible heat, undisturbed, for at least 1½ hours, or until the potatoes are crisp (use a thin spatula to lift a bit of the mixture and peek). At this point you can hold it over minimum heat for another half hour or so, or turn off the heat, then reheat over medium-low heat for 15 minutes before serving. For extra richness, add another 2 tablespoons of butter, cut up, to the rice during the last few minutes of cooking. Serve hot.

Wine: A straightforward white with a little body, like a Pinot Blanc, might be best, but I wouldn't give it too much thought; almost anything white will do.

Serving: Salt-Cured Cod with Arugula Sauce (Meat, Fish & Poultry, page 26)

Grilled Bread Salad

Bread salad is a way of making good use of stale bread. The bread is softened, usually with water, olive oil, lemon juice, or a combination, then tossed with tomatoes and a variety of seasonings. Like many old-fashioned preparations created as a way to salvage food before it goes bad, bread salad has an appeal of its own.

You can wait around for bread to go stale, but the best way to ready bread for salad is to use the grill or broiler to dry the bread quickly while charring the edges slightly. Watch the bread as you grill or broil it; it's a short step to burned bread.

The time you allow the bread to soften after tossing it with the seasonings varies; keep tasting until the texture pleases you. If your tomatoes are on the dry side, you might add extra liquid, in the form of more olive oil and lemon juice, or a light sprinkling of water.

Makes: 4 servings

Time: 45 to 60 minutes (somewhat unattended)

---

1 small baguette (about 8 ounces) or other crusty bread

¼ cup extra virgin olive oil

¼ cup fresh lemon juice (good vinegar also works well)

2 tablespoons diced shallot, scallion, or red onion

¼ teaspoon minced garlic (optional)

1½ pounds tomatoes, chopped

Salt and freshly ground black pepper

¼ cup or more roughly chopped fresh basil or parsley

1. Start a gas or charcoal grill or preheat the broiler; the rack should be 4 to 6 inches from the heat source. Cut the bread lengthwise into quarters. Grill or broil the bread, watching carefully and turning as each side browns and chars slightly; total time will be less than 10 minutes.

2. While the bread cools, mix together the next five ingredients in a large bowl. Mash the tomatoes with the back of a fork to release all of their juices. Season to taste with salt and pepper. Cut the bread into ½- to 1-inch cubes (no larger) and toss with the dressing.

3. Let the bread sit for 20 to 30 minutes, tossing occasionally and tasting a piece every now and then. The salad is at its peak when the bread is fairly soft with some crispy edges, but you can serve it before or after it reaches that state. When it's ready, stir in the herb and serve.

Wine: Red and spicy, like Zinfandel or any of the southern Rhône varietals

Serving: Because it's juicy, almost saucy, and pleasantly acidic, this salad makes a nice accompaniment to simple grilled meat or poultry, and has a special affinity for dark fish such as tuna and swordfish.

Coconut Rice and Beans

Another classic dish, one that, once you master it, will become routine. I never get tired of it.

Makes: 8 servings

Time: 30 minutes

---

3 cans coconut milk, 5 to 6 cups

2½ cups rice, preferably jasmine

Salt

1½ cups moist, cooked (or canned) kidney, pinto, pink, or black beans

1. Combine the coconut milk and rice in a saucepan and bring to a boil over medium heat, stirring occasionally. Add some salt, reduce the heat to low, and cover. Cook for 10 minutes, stirring occasionally to make sure the bottom doesn't stick or burn.

2. Uncover and continue to cook, stirring, over low heat until the rice is tender and the mixture is creamy. If the liquid evaporates before the rice is done, stir in some water, about ½ cup at a time, and cook until done. Stir in the beans about 5 minutes before the rice is finished.

Wine: Beer is most appropriate, but a chilled Pinot Noir or Beaujolais would be terrific.

Serving: Curried Sweet Potato Soup with Apricot (Small Plates & Soups, page 64) and Crispy Pork Bits with Jerk Seasoning (Meat, Fish & Poultry, page 88)

Bread Pudding with Shiitake Mushrooms

This bread casserole is a major upgrade from stuffing.

Makes: 8 servings

Time: About 1 hour, largely unattended

---

2 tablespoons unsalted butter or extra virgin olive oil, plus more for the dish

8 ounces good white bread, cut or torn into chunks no smaller than 1 inch

2 cups milk

4 eggs

Salt and freshly ground black pepper

2 ounces freshly grated Parmesan cheese

4 ounces freshly grated Emmentaler or other semisoft cheese

1 cup sliced shiitake mushrooms (caps only; stems should be reserved for stock or discarded)

1 teaspoon fresh thyme leaves, or ¼ teaspoon dried

1. Butter or oil an 8-inch soufflé or baking dish and put the bread in it. Combine the milk, eggs, salt, pepper, and cheeses and pour this mixture over the bread. Submerge the bread with a weighted plate and turn the oven to 350°F. Meanwhile, heat the butter or oil in a skillet over medium-high heat and sauté the mushrooms, stirring occasionally, until they begin to brown, about 10 minutes. Sprinkle them with the thyme and additional salt and pepper and stir into the bread mixture.

2. Bake until the pudding is just set but not dry, 35 to 45 minutes. The top will be crusty and brown. Serve hot, warm, or at room temperature.

Wine: A Chardonnay or a white Burgundy

Serving: Salmon and Tomatoes Cooked in Foil (Meat, Fish & Poultry, page 10)

Golden Pilaf
with Saffron

This classic rice dish from the eastern Mediterranean, easier than risotto but no less delicious, is largely dependent on the quality of the rice and the stock. Use basmati rice for the best texture.

Makes: 8 servings

Time: 60 minutes, largely unattended

3 cups chicken, beef, or vegetable stock

1 teaspoon saffron threads

4 tablespoons (½ stick) unsalted butter or extra virgin olive oil

1 large onion, chopped

Salt

2 cups white rice, preferably basmati

Freshly ground black pepper

1 cup chopped fresh parsley

¼ cup fresh lemon juice

1. Gently warm the stock with the saffron in a small saucepan while you proceed with the recipe. Put the butter in a large, deep skillet that can later be covered and turn the heat to medium. Add the onion and a large pinch of salt and cook, stirring occasionally, until the onion turns translucent, 5 to 10 minutes. Add the rice and cook, stirring occasionally, until the rice is glossy and begins to brown, 3 to 5 minutes. Season with salt and pepper.

2. Add the warm stock and stir. Raise the heat and bring the mixture to a boil; cook for a minute or two, then reduce the heat to low and cover. Cook for about 15 minutes, or until most of the liquid is absorbed. Turn the heat to the absolute minimum (if you have an electric stove, turn off the heat and let the pan sit on the burner) and let rest another 15 to 30 minutes. Stir in the parsley and lemon juice and serve.

Wine: You can go with a fruity red here, if you like— Pinot Noir, Zinfandel, or something similar—but a crisp, not-too-rich Chardonnay, especially from Chablis, is probably best.

Serving: Roast Striped Bass with Tomatoes and Olives (Meat, Fish & Poultry, page 18)

Pilaf with Pine Nuts and Currants

This familiar pilaf marries the sweetness of currants with the crunch of pine nuts to gain distinction.

Makes: 8 servings

Time: 2 hours

3 cups chicken, beef, or vegetable stock

3 tablespoons unsalted butter or extra virgin olive oil

1 large onion, chopped

Salt

2 cups white rice, preferably basmati

½ cup currants or raisins

¼ cup pine nuts

1 teaspoon ground cinnamon

Freshly ground black pepper

½ cup chopped fresh parsley

1. Gently warm the stock in a small saucepan while you proceed with the recipe. Put the butter in a large, deep skillet that can later be covered and turn the heat to medium. Add the onion and a large pinch of salt and cook, stirring occasionally, until the onion turns translucent, 5 to 10 minutes. Add the rice, currants, pine nuts, and cinnamon and cook, stirring occasionally, until the rice is glossy and begins to brown, 3 to 5 minutes. Season with salt and pepper.

2. Add the warm stock and stir. Raise the heat and bring the mixture to a boil; cook for a minute or two, then reduce the heat to low and cover. Cook for about 15 minutes, or until most of the liquid is absorbed. Turn the heat to the absolute minimum (if you have an electric stove, turn off the heat and let the pan sit on the burner) and let the pilaf rest another 15 to 30 minutes. Stir in the parsley and serve.

Wine: Red and good. It can be an austere Cabernet from Bordeaux or a relatively fruity choice from California.

Serving: Mushroom-Barley Soup (Small Plates & Soups, page 60), Breaded Lamb Cutlets (Meat, Fish & Poultry, page 80), and Tender Spinach and Crisp Shallots (Vegetables, page 39)

Rice Salad
with Peas and Soy

You can use any short- or medium-grain rice you like for this dish, which is most easily made with leftover rice.

Makes: 4 to 6 servings

Time: 30 minutes

½ cup fresh or frozen peas

1 cup Arborio rice

¼ cup minced shallot

¼ cup fresh lime juice, plus more as needed

2 tablespoons peanut, grapeseed, corn, or other neutral oil

2 tablespoons soy sauce

¼ cup minced fresh cilantro

Freshly ground black pepper

1. Bring a small pot of water to a boil; salt it. Bring a large pot of water to a boil; salt it. Cook the peas in the small pot for about 2 minutes, or until they lose their raw flavor. Drain and rinse in cold water to stop the cooking. Drain and set aside.

2. When the large pot of water comes to a boil, add the rice and cook, stirring, until it is completely tender, about 15 minutes. Drain the rice and rinse it quickly under cold water to stop the cooking, but don't chill it entirely.

3. Stir the shallot into the rice and mix well. Add the lime juice, oil, and soy sauce and mix well again. Add the cilantro, peas, and pepper and mix. Taste and add more lime juice, soy sauce, or pepper as needed. Serve immediately or refrigerate, well covered, for up to a day. Bring back to room temperature before serving.

Wine: Beer or not-too-dry Gewürztraminer or Riesling

Serving: Herbed Green Salad with Soy Vinaigrette (Vegetables, page 12)

Garlic-Mushroom Flan

We usually think of custards as desserts, but they may be savory as well, and in that form make luxurious starters or light, flavorful main courses. Custards like garlic flan are often served in top restaurants, but the simplicity and ease of this preparation make them good options for home cooks. Here's one with a surprise in it: cooked shiitakes. It will be a hit.

Makes: 8 servings

Time: 40 minutes

---

2 tablespoons unsalted butter

1 teaspoon minced garlic

1 cup thinly sliced shiitake mushrooms (caps only; stems should be reserved for stock or discarded)

Salt and freshly ground black pepper

3 cups chicken or beef stock

8 eggs

1. Put the butter in a medium saucepan and turn the heat to medium. Add the garlic and mushrooms and cook, stirring occasionally and sprinkling with salt and pepper, until the garlic is fragrant and the mushrooms begin to soften, just 5 minutes or so. Stir in the stock.

2. Beat the eggs lightly in a large bowl and add a bit of the stock mixture. Beat again, then add the remaining stock. Put about an inch of water in a flameproof baking pan or skillet just large enough to hold eight 6-ounce ramekins and turn the heat to high. When the water boils, turn the heat to low, pour the egg mixture into the ramekins, and put the ramekins in the water. Cover tightly with foil and/or a lid.

3. Simmer for 15 to 20 minutes, then check; the moment the custards are set—they should still be quite jiggly—remove them from the water. Serve hot or at room temperature.

Wine: A great white Burgundy, from the area of Montrachet or Meursault, if you can afford it

Serving: Roasted Bay Scallops with Brown Butter and Shallots (Meat, Fish & Poultry, page 28), Endives Braised in Broth with Parmesan (Vegetables, page 34)

Index

About the Author

Mark Bittman created and wrote the weekly *New York Times* column "The Minimalist," which ran for thirteen years. He currently covers food policy and all topics related to eating in a weekly op-ed column for the *New York Times*, and is the lead writer for the *Eat* column in the Sunday *New York Times Magazine*.

Bittman has written more than a dozen cookbooks, including *The Minimalist Cooks at Home*, *The Minimalist Cooks Dinner*, *The Minimalist Entertains*, as well as the popular family of kitchen standards *How to Cook Everything*, *How to Cook Everything Vegetarian*, and *How to Cook Everything The Basics*. Bittman explores global cuisines in *The Best Recipes in the World*, an inspired collection of recipes culled from his international travels. With Jean-Georges Vongerichten, he coauthored *Jean-Georges* (winner of a James Beard Award) and *Simple to Spectacular*. And his bestselling *Food Matters* and *Food Matters Cookbook* offer simple ways to improve your diet and the health of the planet.

As a longtime feature on commercial and public television, Bittman has hosted three award-winning cooking series on PBS, is often invited to share his viewpoints on news and magazine programs, and appears regularly on the *Today* show. He also records a weekly web video for the magazine, revisiting recipes from the beloved Minimalist column. For more information, visit www.markbittman.com.

Notes

 **The Mini Minimalist
Vegetables**

Mark Bittman
The Mini Minimalist

Vegetables

Clarkson Potter/Publishers
New York

Contents

Vegetables

Simple Green Salad

Many people are hooked on premade salad dressing because they believe that homemade dressing is a production, but it need not be. Try this.

Makes: 8 servings

Time: 10 minutes

About 12 cups torn assorted greens

½ cup extra virgin olive oil, more or less

¼ cup balsamic vinegar or sherry vinegar, or fresh lemon juice to taste

Pinch of salt, plus more to taste

Freshly ground black pepper (optional)

Place the greens in a bowl and drizzle them with the oil, vinegar, and a pinch of salt. Toss and taste. Correct the seasoning, add pepper, if desired, and serve immediately.

Wine: Should be determined by the main course

Serving: A great staple for almost any meal in need of a salad

Herbed Green Salad with Nut Vinaigrette

This dressing is not exactly a vinaigrette, since you just toss the oil and some vinegar or lemon juice on the greens. But it does the job beautifully.

Makes: 8 servings

Time: 20 minutes

2 cups assorted chopped mild fresh herbs, like parsley, dill, mint, basil, and/or chervil

¼ cup minced fresh chives

1 teaspoon minced fresh tarragon (optional)

12 cups mesclun or other greens

Salt and freshly ground black pepper

1 cup hazelnut or walnut oil

Sherry vinegar or fresh lemon juice

1. Combine the herbs and greens; cover with a damp towel and refrigerate until ready to serve, not more than a couple of hours.

2. When you're ready to serve, toss the greens with salt, pepper, and the oil. Add vinegar or lemon juice a tablespoon or two at a time, tasting until you are satisfied with the acidity. Add more salt and pepper if necessary and serve.

Wine: Should be determined by the main course

Serving: Another great salad, ideal for a variety of meals

Herbed Green Salad with Soy Vinaigrette

A load of herbs and a strong vinaigrette make this salad special.

Makes: 8 servings

Time: 20 minutes

2 cups assorted chopped mild fresh herbs, like parsley, dill, mint, basil, and/or chervil

¼ cup minced fresh chives

1 teaspoon minced fresh tarragon (optional)

12 cups mesclun or other greens

1 cup grapeseed or olive oil

½ cup fresh lemon juice, or to taste

¼ cup soy sauce

Freshly ground black pepper

Salt (optional)

1. Combine the herbs and greens; cover with a damp towel and refrigerate until ready to serve, not more than a couple of hours.

2. When you're ready to serve, whisk together the oil, lemon juice, soy sauce, and about ½ teaspoon of pepper. Add salt if necessary (it may not be). Toss with the greens, and add more salt or lemon juice if necessary; serve immediately.

Wine: Should be determined by the main course

Serving: This simple salad can be served with most meals.

Big Chopped Salad with Vinaigrette

Please, see this ingredients list as a series of suggestions rather than dogma—a chopped salad can contain any combination that appeals to you, including raw vegetables like broccoli or cauliflower, or crunchy cabbages like bok choi, as well as nuts, seeds, and fruit.

Makes: 8 servings

Time: 30 minutes

---

1 large head romaine lettuce

1 bunch arugula

1 bunch watercress

2 medium cucumbers or 1 English cucumber

1 bunch radishes

2 yellow or red bell peppers

2 carrots

2 celery stalks

1 small sweet onion, like Vidalia

¾ cup extra virgin olive oil

About ⅓ cup good vinegar

1 shallot, minced

1 tablespoon Dijon mustard

Salt and freshly ground black pepper

1. Wash and dry all the vegetables as necessary. Roughly chop the greens and place them in a big bowl.

2. Peel the cucumbers, then cut them in half lengthwise; seed if necessary and chop into ½-inch dice. Trim the radishes and chop into ½-inch dice. Seed and core the peppers and chop into ½-inch dice. Peel the carrots and chop into ½-inch dice. Chop the celery into ½-inch dice. Peel and mince the onion. Toss all the vegetables with the greens.

3. Combine the oil, vinegar, shallot, and mustard and beat with a fork or wire whisk, or emulsify in a blender or with an immersion blender. Season with salt and pepper, then taste and adjust the seasoning as necessary.

4. Just before serving, toss the salad with the dressing.

Wine: Should be determined by the main course

Serving: Another great staple for almost any meal in need of a salad

Pear and Gorgonzola Green Salad with Walnuts

As far a cry from iceberg lettuce and bottled dressing as you can imagine, this is a magical combination of powerful flavors made without cooking or any major challenges.

Simple as this salad is, without top-quality ingredients it won't amount to much. So use sherry or good balsamic vinegar to make the dressing; use pears that are tender and very juicy, not crunchy, mushy, or dry; and use real Italian Gorgonzola. It should be creamy; if you can taste it before buying, so much the better.

This rich salad can serve as the centerpiece of a light lunch, accompanied by little more than bread. It makes an equally great starter for a grand dinner—followed by roasted meat or fish, for example—or a simple one, served with soup.

Makes: 4 servings

Time: 20 minutes

---

2 large pears (about 1 pound)

1 tablespoon fresh lemon juice

1 cup walnuts

¼ pound Gorgonzola or other creamy blue cheese

6 cups mixed greens, torn into bite-size pieces

About ½ cup Basic Vinaigrette (recipe follows)

1. Peel and core the pears; cut them into ½-inch chunks and toss with the lemon juice. Cover and refrigerate for up to 2 hours until needed.

2. Toast the walnuts in a dry skillet over medium heat, shaking the pan frequently, until they are aromatic and beginning to darken, 3 to 5 minutes. Set aside to cool.

3. Crumble the Gorgonzola into small bits; cover and refrigerate until needed.

4. When you're ready to serve, toss the pears, cheese, and greens together with as much of the dressing as you like. Crumble the toasted walnuts over the salad and serve immediately.

Basic Vinaigrette

It's hard to imagine five minutes in the kitchen better spent than those devoted to making vinaigrette, the closest thing to an all-purpose sauce.

The standard ratio for making vinaigrette is three parts oil to one part vinegar, but because the vinegars I use are mild and extra virgin olive oil is quite assertive, I usually wind up at about two parts oil to one part vinegar, or even a little stronger. Somewhere in that range you're going to find a home for your own taste; start by using a ratio of three to one and taste, adding more vinegar until you're happy. (You may even prefer more vinegar than olive oil; there's nothing wrong with that.)

Be sure to use good wine vinegar; balsamic and sherry vinegars, while delicious, are too dominant for some salads, fine for others. Lemon juice is a fine substitute, but because it is less acidic than most vinegars—3 or 4 percent compared to 6 or 7 percent—you will need more of it.

The ingredients may be combined with a spoon, fork, whisk, or blender. Hand tools give you an unconvincing emulsion that must be used immediately. Blenders produce vinaigrettes that very much resemble thin mayonnaise in color and thickness—without using egg. They also dispose of the job of mincing the shallot; just peel, chop, and dump it into the container at the last minute (if you add it earlier, it will be pureed, depriving you of the pleasure of its distinctive crunch).

This is best made fresh but will keep, refrigerated, for a few days. Bring it back to room temperature and whisk briefly before using it.

Makes: About ⅔ cup

Time: 10 minutes

½ cup extra virgin olive oil

3 tablespoons good-quality wine vinegar,
or more to taste

Salt and freshly ground black pepper

1 heaping teaspoon Dijon mustard

1 large shallot (about 1 ounce), peeled and cut into chunks

1. Combine all ingredients except the shallot in a blender and turn the machine on; a creamy emulsion will form within 30 seconds. Taste and add more vinegar, a teaspoon or two at a time, until the balance tastes right to you.

2. Add the shallot and turn the machine on and off a few times until the shallot is minced within the dressing. Taste, adjust the seasoning, and serve.

Wine: Should be determined by the main course

Serving: Works well as a dressing with most green salads

Tomato Salad with Basil

So few ingredients, and so much flavor—as long as the ingredients are of high quality! Omit the basil if you can't find any, but where there are good tomatoes there is probably good basil. Add slices of mozzarella to make this more substantial.

Makes: 4 servings

Time: 10 minutes

4 perfectly ripe medium tomatoes

Salt and freshly ground black pepper

A handful of washed, dried, and roughly chopped basil

Extra virgin olive oil

1. Core the tomatoes (cut a cone-shaped wedge out of the stem end) and cut them into slices about ¼ inch thick.

2. Lay the tomatoes on a platter or 4 individual plates. Sprinkle with salt, pepper, and basil. Drizzle with oil and serve.

Wine: Should be determined by the main course.

Serving: This summer salad can be served with Grilled Steaks with Roquefort Sauce (Meat, Fish & Poultry, page 62) and Fennel with Olive Oil Dipping Sauce (page 38).

Simple Cucumber Salad

Many cucumbers are best if they're salted first. The process removes some of their bitterness and makes them extra-crisp— it takes some time but almost no effort. Start with one or two Kirby (pickling) cucumbers per person—or half of a medium cucumber or about a third of a long ("English") cucumber.

Makes: 4 servings

Time: 1 hour, largely unattended

About 1½ pounds cucumbers, peeled and thinly sliced

Salt

½ cup coarsely chopped and loosely packed fresh mint or dill

Juice of ½ lemon

Freshly ground black pepper

1. Put the cucumber slices in a colander and sprinkle with salt, just a little more than if you were planning to eat them right away. Set the colander in the sink.

2. After 30 to 45 minutes, press the cucumbers to extract as much liquid as possible. Toss them with the mint, the lemon juice, and a healthy grinding of black pepper. Serve within a few hours.

Wine: Should be determined by the main course

Serving: Makes an excellent summer salad with a grilled meal

Seaweed Salad with Cucumber

This is simply a kind of sea-based mesclun with a distinctively sesame-flavored dressing. You can use leftover chicken (or shrimp) or cook it expressly for this purpose; start with about a pound of boneless chicken or shrimp and steam, grill, broil, roast, or pan-grill until done, less than ten minutes. (You can also omit the chicken or shrimp entirely; the salad is delicious without it.)

To toast sesame seeds, heat them in a dry skillet over medium heat, shaking occasionally, until they brown lightly and begin to pop.

Makes: 8 servings

Time: 20 minutes

2 ounces wakame or assorted seaweeds

1 pound cucumbers, preferably Kirby, English, or Japanese

1 pound shredded cooked chicken or roughly chopped cooked shrimp (optional)

½ cup minced shallots, scallions, or red onion

¼ cup soy sauce

2 tablespoons rice wine or other light vinegar

2 tablespoons mirin

2 tablespoons toasted sesame oil

½ teaspoon cayenne, or to taste

Salt, if necessary

2 tablespoons toasted sesame seeds (optional)

1. Rinse the seaweed once and soak it in at least ten times its volume of water.

2. Wash and dice the cucumbers; do not peel unless necessary. When the seaweed is tender, 5 minutes later, drain and gently squeeze the mixture to remove the excess water. Pick through the seaweed to sort out any hard bits (there may be none), and chop or cut up (you can use scissors, which you may find easier) if the pieces are large. Combine the cucumber and seaweed mixture in a bowl; add the chicken or shrimp (if desired) to the bowl.

3. Toss with the remaining ingredients except the sesame seeds; taste and add salt or other seasonings as necessary, and serve, garnished with the sesame seeds, if using.

Wine: A not-perfectly-dry Riesling

Serving: Chawan-Mushi (Small Plates & Soups, page 20) and white or brown rice for a Japanese-inspired meal

Beet Roesti
with Rosemary

This thick beet pancake, cooked slowly on both sides until the beet sugars caramelize, sports a crunchy, sweet crust that, I swear, is reminiscent of crème brûlée.

Keys to Success

» Beets bleed, as you know. Peel them over the sink, and wash the grater or food processor as soon as you're done with it, and you won't have any serious consequences. Still, you might wear an apron.

» The grating disk of food processors processes the beets quickly and easily, but a box grater works well also.

» The roesti must be cooked in a nonstick skillet, preferably a large one measuring twelve inches across. (If you only have a ten-inch skillet, decrease the amount of beets in the recipe from two pounds to one and a half pounds; the quantity given for other ingredients remain the same.)

» Keep the heat moderate: Too quick-cooking will burn the sugary outside of the pancake while leaving the inside raw.

Makes: 4 to 6 servings

Time: 30 minutes

---

2 pounds beets (about 3 very large or 4 to 6 medium)

2 teaspoons coarsely chopped fresh rosemary

Salt and freshly ground black pepper

½ cup flour

2 tablespoons unsalted butter or extra virgin olive oil

Minced fresh parsley or a few rosemary leaves

1. Trim the beets and peel them as you would potatoes; grate them in a food processor or by hand. Begin preheating a 12-inch nonstick skillet over medium heat.

2. Toss the grated beets in a bowl with the chopped rosemary, salt, and pepper. Add about half the flour; toss well, add the rest of the flour, then toss again.

3. Put the butter in the skillet and heat until it begins to turn nut-brown. Scrape the beet mixture into the skillet and press it down with a spatula to form a round. With the heat at medium to medium-high—the pancake should be sizzling gently—cook, shaking the pan occasionally, until the bottom of the beet cake is nicely crisp, 8 to 10 minutes. Slide the cake out onto a plate, top with another plate, invert the two plates, and return the cake to the pan. Continue to

cook, adjusting the heat if necessary, until the second side is browned, another 10 minutes or so. Garnish with the herb, cut into wedges, and serve hot or at room temperature.

Variations

Beet Salad with Vinaigrette

You don't need to cook the grated beets; simply toss them, raw, with any vinaigrette. Given their sweetness, a strong, harsh vinaigrette, with a high percentage of vinegar, is best.

Wine: Should be determined by the main course

Serving: A stunning side dish for hearty roasted or braised meat dishes, this also makes a good centerpiece for a light meal.

Raw Beet Salad

Use young, small beets if you can find them. And wear an apron or old clothes; you will inevitably spatter some juice.

Makes: 8 servings

Time: 20 minutes

2 pounds beets, preferably small

2 large shallots

Salt and freshly ground black pepper

1 tablespoon Dijon mustard, or to taste

2 tablespoons extra virgin olive oil

¼ cup sherry vinegar or other good strong vinegar

Minced fresh parsley, dill, chervil, rosemary, or tarragon

1. Peel the beets and the shallots. Combine them in the bowl of a food processor fitted with the metal blade, and pulse carefully just until the beets are chopped; do not puree. (Or grate the beets by hand and mince the shallots; combine.) Scrape into a bowl.

2. Toss with the salt, pepper, mustard, oil, and vinegar. Taste and adjust the seasoning. Toss in the herbs and serve.

Wine: A crisp white is best, like a Chablis or comparable California Chardonnay, or even something lighter, like Pinot Grigio.

Serving: Sautéed Red Snapper with Rhubarb Sauce (Meat, Fish & Poultry, page 16) and New Potatoes with Butter and Mint (page 72)

Green Beans
with Tomatoes

This dish of slow-cooked green beans yields soft and sweet beans. It is a perfect side dish for a midwinter meal because it does not depend on sun-ripened tomatoes or crisp just-picked beans for its appeal.

Makes: 4 servings

Time: At least 1 hour, largely unattended

---

2 tablespoons extra virgin olive oil

1 pound green beans, trimmed

1 pint cherry or grape tomatoes

Salt and freshly ground black pepper

1. Put 1 tablespoon of the olive oil in a large skillet and turn the heat to high. Add the beans and cook, undisturbed, until they begin to brown a little on the bottom. Add the tomatoes, turn the heat to low, and cover. Cook for about an hour, stirring occasionally, until the beans are very tender. (You can cook even more slowly if you like, or cook until done, turn off the heat, and reheat gently just before serving.)

2. Season with salt and pepper and stir in the remaining olive oil. Serve hot or at room temperature.

Wine: Depends on the main course

Serving: This midwinter side dish pairs well with Cod with Chickpeas and Sherry (Meat, Fish & Poultry, page 24) and 60-Minute Bread (Pizza, Pasta & Grains, page 72).

Green Beans with Lemon

There is one technique for cooking vegetables that is almost infallible, and works for almost every vegetable you can think of. You precook the vegetables—this is something you can do twenty minutes before you eat or twenty-four hours in advance—and then chill them. At the last minute, you reheat them in butter or oil (or, if you're especially fat-conscious, a dry nonstick skillet). That's it. The advantages are numerous. You can precook a lot of vegetables at once, using the same water for each. You can store them and then cook as much as you need when you need it. You can finish the cooking in five minutes. And the technique is foolproof. I use green beans as an example, but this is as close to a generic recipe as there is; it will work with any vegetable that is suitable for cooking in water—beets, potatoes, turnips, broccoli, greens, cauliflower, fennel, snow peas, shell peas, carrots, or cabbage, to name just a few.

Makes: 4 servings

Time: 20 minutes

1 pound green beans, trimmed

1 to 2 tablespoons extra virgin olive oil or unsalted butter, or a combination

1 lemon

1. Bring a large pot of water to a boil and salt it; add the beans and cook until bright green and tender, about 5 minutes. Do not overcook.

2. Drain the beans, then plunge them into a large bowl filled with ice water to stop the cooking. When they're cool, drain again. Cover and refrigerate for up to a couple of days, or proceed.

3. Zest the lemon and julienne or mince the zest. Juice the lemon. Place the oil and/or butter in a large skillet and turn the heat to medium-high. Add the beans and cook, tossing or stirring, until they are hot and glazed, 3 to 5 minutes. Toss in a serving bowl with the lemon juice, top with the zest, and serve.

Wine: Should be determined by the main course

Serving: This is a classic side dish, useful in accompanying almost any main course.

Steamed Broccoli with Beurre Noisette

Beurre noisette is brown, or nut-colored, butter, a French classic that fully qualifies as a sauce yet contains only one ingredient. If you've never had it, beurre noisette's complex flavor and beguiling aroma, redolent of hazelnuts, will amaze you. And if you like it over broccoli, you'll probably find that you like it over almost any other sturdy, full-flavored vegetable.

Makes: 4 servings

Time: 20 minutes

---

1 pound broccoli

3 tablespoons butter

Salt and freshly ground black pepper

½ to 1 tablespoon fresh lemon juice

1. Trim the broccoli as necessary (peel the thick stems with a vegetable peeler or paring knife to make them less tough). Cut into equal-size pieces.

2. Put the butter in a small saucepan over medium heat. Cook, swirling the pan occasionally, until the butter stops foaming and begins to brown. Remove from the heat immediately and season lightly with salt and pepper; keep warm if necessary.

3. Steam the broccoli over boiling water (or boil in salted water to cover) until tender and bright green, usually less than 10 minutes. Drain if necessary and sprinkle with salt. (Or run under cold water and refrigerate. To reheat, put a little olive oil or butter in a pan over medium heat and turn the broccoli in it until hot.) Swirl the lemon juice into the beurre noisette and drizzle it over the broccoli; serve immediately.

Wine: Should be determined by the main course

Serving: A great staple side dish for a quick weeknight meal; try pairing with Fastest Roast Chicken (Meat, Fish & Poultry, page 43) and 60-Minute Bread (Pizza, Pasta & Grains, page 72).

Endives Braised in Broth with Parmesan

Grown indoors in the dark, endives are among the perfect winter vegetables, usually used in salads but also lovely when cooked. This simple gratin benefits from good, dark stock, but the addition of Parmigiano-Reggiano will cover you if you resort to canned stock.

Makes: 4 servings

Time: 40 minutes

---

4 whole Belgian endives

1 cup good-quality stock

Salt and freshly ground black pepper

¼ cup freshly grated Parmigiano-Reggiano cheese

1. Remove just a couple of the outer leaves from each of the endives; rinse them and put them in a skillet in one layer. Add the stock and sprinkle with salt and pepper. Cover and cook over medium heat until tender, 20 to 30 minutes. Preheat the broiler.

2. Cover the endives with the cheese and run under the broiler, just long enough to slightly brown the cheese. Serve with a slotted spoon.

Wine: A white Burgundy, preferably from the area of Montrachet or Meursault

Serving: Garlic Mushroom Flan (Pizza, Pasta & Grains, page 88) and Roasted Bay Scallops with Brown Butter and Shallots (Meat, Fish & Poultry, page 28)

Fennel Gratin

This is an almost universal technique for vegetables, an honest, simple gratin with a topping of just a couple of ingredients. Since one of them is rich, flavorful blue cheese, butter isn't even included. My vegetable of choice here is fennel—an underappreciated and almost always available bulb—but you could put this topping on almost any vegetable.

For the cheese, you can use Gorgonzola, the soft Italian cheese; bleu d'Auvergne, a mild cheese from France; Maytag blue, the premier domestic variety; Stilton, the classic English blue; or Roquefort, which is made from sheep's milk. All are good, but my preference is for the stronger cheeses, such as Roquefort and Maytag.

The bread crumbs are best when freshly made from good but slightly stale bread; coarse bread crumbs, such as those made in a food processor, are infinitely preferable to the finer store-bought variety.

Makes: 4 servings

Time: 20 minutes

---

1 fennel bulb (about 1 pound)

½ cup coarse bread crumbs

¼ cup crumbled blue cheese

Freshly ground black pepper

1. Preheat the oven to 400°F. Bring a small pot of water to a boil.

2. Trim the fennel, then cut it into about ¼-inch-thick slices and cook in the boiling water until just tender, less than 5 minutes. Drain and layer

in a shallow baking dish. (You can also drain the vegetables, then stop their cooking by plunging them into ice water, then drain again. In this manner you can finish the cooking up to a day or two later; increase the baking time to 20 minutes.)

3. Top the fennel with the bread crumbs, then the cheese; season all with pepper to taste (hold off on salt, because the cheese is salty). Bake until the cheese melts, about 10 minutes.

4. Run the baking dish under the broiler until the top browns, checking every 30 seconds. Serve hot or at room temperature.

Variations

Almost any vegetable will work here; some must be parboiled: green beans, broccoli, cauliflower, leeks, celery, etc. Some need not be (see Roasted Asparagus with Parmesan, page 45): thin asparagus, zucchini, sliced tomatoes.

The flavoring can be changed by varying the cheese. Or toss a couple of tablespoons of minced parsley in with the bread crumbs, or a tiny bit (½ teaspoon or so) of minced garlic.

Wine: A good, solid red—Cabernet or one of the Rhône varietals—would probably be best.

Serving: A side dish, for sure, but one that can dominate the table; serve it with plain broiled chicken or fish.

Fennel with Olive Oil Dipping Sauce

Fennel remains exotic enough to be a treat for many people, and this simple preparation simply elevates its stature a bit. Trim and discard the hard, hollow stalks that jut out from the top of the bulb; if you get your hands on a bulb with its fronds still attached, roughly chop them and add them to the hot oil with the garlic.

Makes: 4 servings

Time: 15 minutes

¼ cup extra virgin olive oil

1 garlic clove, peeled and lightly crushed

Salt and freshly ground black pepper

Zest of ½ lemon, minced

½ fennel bulb, trimmed and cut into strips

1. Combine half the olive oil with the garlic in a small saucepan and turn the heat to medium-low. Cook, shaking the pan occasionally, until the garlic begins to sizzle. Remove the garlic from the oil and the pan from the heat.

2. Add the cold oil to the hot, along with salt, pepper, and lemon zest. Serve the fennel with the dipping sauce.

Wine: A sprightly red, like a Beaujolais, or a lighter Côtes du Rhône, preferably chilled

Serving: Grilled Steaks with Roquefort Sauce (Meat, Fish & Poultry, page 62) and 60-Minute Bread (Pizza, Pasta & Grains, page 72)

Tender Spinach and Crisp Shallots

There are a number of ways to make simple dishes of greens more appealing. Among my favorites is to prepare a topping of crisp-fried shallots. By themselves, these are irresistible; when combined with tender greens they create an alluring contrast in flavor and texture. Furthermore, the oil in which the shallots have been fried is a great addition to the greens and, in the days following, to many other dishes.

The shallots must be thinly sliced, and this is the perfect occasion to use mandolin if you have one. If you do not, just peel, then slice them as thinly as you can, using a small, sharp knife.

This preparation also serves as a good introduction to deep-frying, because the watchful eye can readily and infallibly detect when the shallots are ready—they turn brown. At that moment, they must be removed from the heat immediately or they will burn. The deliciously flavored oil should be strained and stored in the refrigerator; it can be used in vinaigrette or in cooking.

Makes: 4 servings

Time: 30 minutes

½ cup or more neutral oil, like grapeseed or corn

5 large shallots (½ pound or more), thinly sliced

Salt and freshly ground black pepper

1 pound spinach

1. Put the oil in a small to medium saucepan or narrow skillet at least an inch deep. Turn the heat to high and wait a few minutes; the oil should reach 350°F. (If you do not have a frying thermometer, just drop in a couple slices of shallot; when the oil around them bubbles vigorously, it's ready.)

2. Add the shallots and cook, adjusting the heat so that the bubbling is vigorous but not explosive. Cook, stirring, until the shallots begin to darken, 8 to 12 minutes. As soon as they turn golden brown, remove them immediately with a slotted spoon—be careful, because overcooking at this point will burn the shallots. Drain the shallots on paper towels and sprinkle with salt and pepper; they'll keep for a couple of hours this way.

3. Meanwhile, bring a large pot of water to a boil and salt it. When it is ready, add the spinach and cook until it wilts, about 1 minute. Remove the spinach with a strainer or slotted spoon and plunge it into a large bowl filled with ice water to stop the cooking. When it's cool, drain and chop. (You can store the spinach, covered and refrigerated, for up to a couple of days if you like.)

4. Place 1 tablespoon of the shallot oil in a skillet and turn the heat to medium-high. Add the spinach and cook, stirring frequently and breaking up any clumps, until hot, about 5 minutes. Season with salt and pepper and serve, topped with the crisp shallots.

Variations

You can use any leafy green you like here. Some, like collards and kale, will take up to 10 minutes to soften in the boiling water; just keep testing for doneness (sampling) until you're satisfied that they're tender. (Thick stems of ¼ inch or more will take even longer; start them in the water a few minutes before adding the greens.)

Wine: Depending on the center-of-the-plate preparation, a full-bodied Chardonnay is a likely candidate.

Serving: Use this as a bed for simply broiled chicken or fish and it becomes a whole meal.

Grilled Asparagus with Lemon Dressing

This preparation favors thick spears of asparagus, which become tender and remain moist inside while their exteriors char. Those that weigh an ounce or two each—that is, eight to sixteen per pound—are the best. The only difference between thick and pencil asparagus is that thick asparagus must be peeled before cooking to remove the relatively tough skin; use a vegetable peeler or paring knife.

If you are grilling, the simplest thing to do is to pick a sturdy fish that can be grilled without falling apart, such as tuna, monkfish, or swordfish. Any of these can be lightly oiled, seasoned, and slapped on a grill, to be cooked in about the same time as the asparagus. Use the same dressing for the fish.

Makes: 4 servings

Time: 20 minutes

1½ to 2 pounds thick asparagus

About 2 tablespoons extra virgin olive oil

Salt and freshly ground black pepper

Juice of 3 lemons

2 tablespoons minced shallot or scallion

¼ cup minced fresh parsley

1. Snap off the woody ends of the asparagus; most spears will break naturally an inch or two above the bottom. Peel the stalks up to the flower bud. Meanwhile, start a grill or preheat a cast-iron or other heavy skillet over medium-high heat until it smokes.

2. If cooking the asparagus on a grill, toss the spears with about 1 tablespoon of the oil, mixing with your hands until they're coated. Season well with salt and pepper to taste. Grill until tender and browned in spots, turning once or twice, a total of 5 to 10 minutes.

» If cooking the asparagus in a skillet, do not oil or season them. Just toss them in the hot skillet and cook, turning the individual spears as they brown, until tender, 5 to 10 minutes. Remove as they finish and season with salt and pepper.

3. Mix together the lemon juice and shallot, then stir in enough olive oil to add a little body and take the edge off the sharpness of the lemon; the mixture should still be quite strong. Season it with salt and plenty of black pepper and stir in the parsley. Serve the asparagus hot or at room temperature with grilled or broiled swordfish, monkfish, or other sturdy fish. Spoon the sauce over all.

Variation

Asparagus with Soy-Ginger Dressing

Combine ¼ cup soy sauce with 1½ teaspoon minced garlic, 1 teaspoon
minced fresh ginger, ½ teaspoon sugar, 2 teaspoons rice or other mild
vinegar, and a few drops of sesame oil. Serve over the asparagus.

Wine: White and crisp, like Sauvignon Blanc or
Pinot Grigio

Serving: Perfect to serve with tuna, swordfish,
monkfish or any other sturdy fish

Roasted Asparagus with Parmesan

There are two things I love about pencil-thin asparagus: one is that it requires no peeling, because its outer sheath is far more tender than that of its thick cousin; the other is that it cooks much faster. This is especially important when you turn to methods other than boiling or steaming—most notably roasting. What I like to do is roast thin spears until they're just about tender, then top them with a foolproof two-ingredient topping: coarse bread crumbs and Parmigiano-Reggiano cheese. Run that under the broiler, and you get roasted asparagus with a crunchy, high-impact crust.

Keys to Success

» Although I do think real Parmesan is best—especially if you combine it with butter—pecorino or other hard sheep's cheese does a nice job. Use coarse bread crumbs if possible; they might look slightly less attractive, but will give you more crunch.

» Keep an eye on the dish while it's under the broiler—the time needed there is only a minute or two.

Makes: 4 servings

Time: 25 minutes

---

1 thick slice good-quality bread (about 1 ounce)

1 small chunk Parmigiano-Reggiano cheese (about 1 ounce)

About 1½ pounds thin asparagus

3 tablespoons unsalted butter, extra virgin olive oil, or a combination

Salt and freshly ground black pepper

1. Preheat the oven to 500°F; while it's preheating, set the bread on the oven rack and check it frequently until it is lightly toasted and dry. Coarsely grind or grate the bread and cheese together (a small food processor is perfect for this)—if possible, keep the crumbs from becoming as fine as commercial bread crumbs.

2. Rinse the asparagus and break off the woody ends. Lay them in a baking dish that will accommodate them in two or three layers. Toss with bits of the butter and/or oil, sprinkle lightly with salt and pepper, and put in the oven.

3. Roast for 5 minutes, then shake the pan to redistribute the butter or oil. Roast for another 5 minutes, then test the asparagus for doneness by piercing a spear with the point of a sharp knife; it is done when the knife enters the asparagus but still meets a little resistance.

» You can prepare the recipe in advance to this point up to a couple of hours before serving; allow the asparagus to sit at room temperature during that time.

4. Turn on the broiler and put the rack as close as possible to the heating element. Sprinkle the asparagus with the crumbs and carefully brown the top—it will take only a minute or two. Serve the asparagus hot or at room temperature.

Variations

Roasted Asparagus with Garlic
Forget the topping; just toss the asparagus with 1 tablespoon minced garlic at the same time as you add the butter or olive oil.

Roasted Asparagus with Soy and Sesame
Use 1 tablespoon peanut oil in place of the olive oil or butter. Halfway through the roasting, add 1 tablespoon soy sauce to the asparagus. Top with about 2 tablespoons sesame seeds; run under the broiler until they begin to pop, about 1 minute. Finish with a sprinkling of soy sauce, just a teaspoon or two.

Wine: Any dry white

Serving: This flavorful side dish will overshadow nearly anything you serve on the center of the plate, so keep it simple—grilled or broiled meat or fish, perhaps with some lemon.

Stir-Fried Leeks
with Ginger

A big deal is often made of washing leeks—they can be very sandy—but since you're going to be chopping these, it's easy.

Makes: 4 servings

Time: 30 minutes

2 large leeks (about 1½ pounds)

2 tablespoons peanut or olive oil

2 tablespoons minced peeled fresh ginger

Salt and freshly ground black pepper

1½ teaspoons soy sauce

1. Cut off the last couple of inches of dark green leaves, those without any pale green core, from the leeks. Then stand each leek on its tail and use a sharp knife to "shave" the remaining bits of tough, dark green leaves off the stalk. When only white and pale green leaves remain, cut off the root, slice the leeks in half (or, if they're large, into quarters), and chop them roughly. Then wash in a salad spinner (or a colander inserted into a large bowl) until no traces of sand remain and spin or pat dry.

2. Put the oil in a large skillet, preferably nonstick, and turn the heat to high. When a bit of smoke appears, add the leeks, all at once. Let sit for a couple of minutes, then cook, stirring only occasionally, for about 10 minutes.

3. When the leeks dry out and begin to brown, sprinkle with the ginger. Cook, stirring for 2 or 3 minutes, then add some salt (just a little) and pepper, along with the soy sauce. Taste and adjust the seasoning, then serve.

Wine: A light, dry white like Pinot Blanc, or a dry rosé from Provence or elsewhere

Serving: Herbed Green Salad with Soy Vinaigrette (page 12), Vietnamese-Style Pork (Meat, Fish & Poultry, page 85), and white or brown rice

Grilled Red Peppers with Olive Oil and Sherry Vinegar

The standard grilled pepper should be a part of every home cook's repertoire. They're a perfect accompaniment to nearly any simply grilled dish. Feel free to use a mix of yellow, orange, and red bell peppers if it appeals to you.

Makes: 4 servings

Time: 30 minutes

---

4 large red bell peppers (about 2 pounds)

2 tablespoons extra virgin olive oil

1 tablespoon sherry vinegar

1 tablespoon drained capers (optional)

Salt and freshly ground black pepper

1. Start a grill or preheat the broiler; put the rack about 4 inches from the heat source. When the fire is hot, put the peppers directly over the heat. Grill, turning as each side blackens, until they collapse, about 15 minutes. Wrap in foil and let cool until you can handle them, then remove the skin, seeds, and stems. You will inevitably shred them in this process, and that's fine.

2. Drizzle the peppers with the olive oil and vinegar, then sprinkle with the capers if you like and some pepper. Taste and add salt if necessary, then serve.

Wine: Anything from Zinfandel to chilled Beaujolais

Serving: Herbed Green Salad with Nut Vinaigrette (page 11), Grilled Steaks with Roquefort Sauce (Meat, Fish & Poultry, page 62), and Grilled Corn (page 64)

Piquillo Peppers
with Shiitakes and Spinach

Pimientos del piquillo—piquillo peppers—are the brilliant crimson, cone-shaped peppers from Navarre, a region of western Spain. You couldn't bioengineer a better shape for stuffing, and there's no preparation involved, because piquillo peppers are sold only in cans or bottles. All of this adds up to a terrific "new" ingredient for home cooks. Here they're stuffed with shiitakes and spinach, an easy preparation. But you can use almost any stuffing you like, or you can sauté the piquillos unstuffed; they're great that way.

The best piquillos are from a town called Lodosa, and are so labeled. They are harvested by hand, then roasted over wood and hand-peeled—no water is allowed to touch them, for this would wash away some of the essential flavors—and canned or bottled with no other ingredients. This regal treatment makes top-quality peppers expensive, about fifteen dollars per pound, but there are alternatives: Some Lodosa peppers are roasted over gas, some have citric acid added as a mild preservative, and there are also piquillo-style peppers from other parts of Spain.

Makes: 4 servings

Time: About 30 minutes

½ cup extra virgin olive oil

2 garlic cloves, peeled and sliced

1 dried hot red chile

2 cups stemmed shiitake mushrooms, thinly sliced or chopped

1 cup cooked spinach, squeezed dry and chopped

Salt and freshly ground black pepper

12 piquillo peppers

1. Place the olive oil in a large skillet, turn the heat to medium, and add the garlic and chile. Cook, stirring occasionally, until the garlic browns lightly, about 5 minutes. Remove the chile and add the shiitakes. Cook, stirring occasionally, until the shiitakes release their liquid and become tender, about 10 minutes. Stir in the spinach and season to taste.

2. Stuff each of the peppers with a portion of this mixture. Serve at room temperature or warm gently in a 250°F oven for about 15 minutes.

Variations

Sautéed Piquillos

Place 2 tablespoons extra virgin olive oil in a large skillet, turn the heat to medium-low, and add 2 teaspoons peeled and slivered garlic. Cook, shaking the pan occasionally, until the garlic turns light brown, about 5 minutes. Add 8 to 12 piquillo peppers and cook just until the peppers begin to change color on the bottom; turn and repeat. Season and serve hot or at room temperature drizzled, if you like, with a little more olive oil and some sherry vinegar.

Piquillos with Anchovies
No cooking here, just place an anchovy fillet in each pepper and drizzle with olive oil, then serve.

Piquillo Bruschetta
Toast a few rounds of good bread; rub each with a cut clove of garlic and top with a piquillo, or if the bread is small, half a piquillo. Drizzle with olive oil and serve.

Other stuffing suggestions for piquillo peppers

» Spinach or other greens sautéed with raisins and pine nuts

» Cooked and chopped tender fish fillets (such as cod or salmon), tossed with chopped tomatoes and a little oil and vinegar

» Stewed and chopped or shredded meat

» Rice bound with a little mayonnaise and chopped shrimp or chicken (good served cold)

Wine: Rioja or another soft, rich red

Serving: Generally, you'd serve these as a main course for a light meal, with salad and bread.

Roast Tomato Frittata

Roast tomatoes, the essential ingredient in this frittata, are great by themselves, in salsas and sauces, or as a garnish for grilled or roasted fish or meat. To serve, cut the frittata into cubes or small slices to make for easy handling; it's better eaten with toothpicks or straight from the hand than with a fork and knife.

Makes: 8 servings

Time: 30 minutes

12 plum tomatoes

¼ cup extra virgin olive oil

4 garlic cloves

Several thyme sprigs

Salt

4 small fingerling potatoes or 1 medium thin-skinned potato

4 small onions or 1 large onion

3 tablespoons unsalted butter or extra virgin olive oil

8 eggs

½ cup freshly grated Parmesan

½ cup minced fresh parsley leaves

Freshly ground black pepper

1. Preheat the oven to 500°F. Core the tomatoes (cut a small, cone-shaped wedge from their stem ends), cut them in half, and use a paring knife or spoon to scoop out the seeds and pulp. Spread about half the oil on a nonstick baking sheet that will accommodate the tomatoes adequately without crowding, then add the tomatoes. Distribute the garlic and thyme among the tomatoes; drizzle with the remaining oil and some salt. Roast, turning the pan in the oven once for even cooking, for about 30 minutes, or until the tomatoes are shriveled and a little blackened. Remove from the oven and cool while you proceed with the recipe.

2. Lower the oven temperature to 350°F. Wash the potatoes (peeling isn't necessary) and cut them into slices somewhat less than ¼ inch thick. Peel the onions. If they're small just cut them in half; if larger, into small wedges.

3. Put the butter in a 10-inch ovenproof skillet, preferably nonstick, and turn the heat to medium-high. When the butter melts, add the potatoes and onions and cook, stirring only occasionally, until the potatoes are nicely browned on both sides. Meanwhile, lightly beat the eggs in a bowl; stir in the Parmesan and parsley, along with some salt and pepper.

4. When the potatoes are ready, turn the heat to low and wait a minute, then add the eggs. If necessary, move the solids around so they are evenly distributed in the egg mixture. Cook until the frittata is set on the edges, then transfer to the oven and bake until the mixture is barely set on top. Serve in wedges, with tomatoes, hot or at room temperature.

Wine: A hearty but simple red, like an inexpensive Côtes du Rhône

Serving: For a light meal, 60-Minute Bread (Pizza, Pasta & Grains, page 72) and Big Chopped Salad with Vinaigrette (page 14)

Roasted Red Peppers

Roasting gives amazing depth to vegetables, especially peppers.
The simplest way to serve these is to drizzle them with extra virgin
olive oil, along with some salt and pepper, but you can also add
a few drops of vinegar. The next step is to garnish with anchovies,
capers, and/or herbs.

Makes: 4 servings

Time: About 1 hour largely unattended

4 large red bell peppers (about 2 pounds)

Salt and freshly ground black pepper

2 tablespoons extra virgin olive oil

1. Preheat the oven to 500°F. Line a roasting pan with enough foil to later fold over the top. Put the peppers in the pan and the pan in the oven. Roast, turning the peppers about every 10 minutes, until the peppers collapse, about 40 minutes.

2. Fold the foil over the peppers and allow them to cool. Working over a bowl, remove the core, skin, and seeds from each of the peppers. It's okay if the peppers naturally fall into strips during this process. Sprinkle with salt, pepper, and olive oil and serve at room temperature. (You can refrigerate these, tightly wrapped or covered, for a few days; bring to room temperature before serving.)

Wine: Should be determined by the main course

Serving: These are a nice accompaniment to most simple meals.

Chipotle-Peach Salsa

Chiles in adobo are chipotles (wood-smoked jalapeños) in a kind of tomato sauce, sold in cans. They're available at any market with a good selection of Mexican foods. If you can't find them, substitute a hot chili powder or even cayenne. Use a pineapple or nectarines instead of peaches, if you prefer.

Makes: About 4 cups

Time: 15 minutes, plus time to rest

4 cups ¼-inch diced peaches

1 cup ¼-inch diced red bell pepper, stemmed and seeded

2 chiles in adobo, pureed

¼ cup fresh lime juice

½ cup minced cilantro

2 tablespoons sugar

Combine all the ingredients and let them "marry" for up to 1 hour before serving.

Wine: Depends on the main course

Serving: Serve with tortilla chips for dipping or as a sauce for grilled or broiled chicken.

Glazed Carrots

This is my favorite way of making a side of carrots to go with a meal. Part of its appeal is its ease and quickness; the other is how easy it is to vary. You can add almost any flavoring you like to these carrots during their final minutes in the pan, like a healthy grating of lemon or orange zest, a tablespoon of grated ginger, or a clove of minced garlic, to suit your taste.

Makes: 4 servings

Time: About 30 minutes

1 pound carrots,
cut into chunks

Salt

2 tablespoons unsalted
butter

Chopped parsley, chervil,
or mint (optional)

1. Put the carrots in a saucepan with a pinch of salt and water to come about halfway up their height. Add the butter, cover the pan, and turn the heat to medium-high. Simmer until the carrots are nearly tender, about 20 minutes.

2. Uncover; much of the water will have evaporated. Continue to cook until the carrots are shiny, about 5 minutes longer; if they threaten to burn, add a tablespoon or two of water. When the carrots are done, taste and adjust the seasoning if necessary, garnish with an herb if you like, and serve.

Wine: Should be determined by the main course.

Serving: Try pairing with Crisp Roasted Rack of Lamb (Meat, Fish & Poultry, page 72) and Pan-Crisped Potatoes (page 68).

Grilled White-and-Sweet Potato Salad

This sharply flavored potato salad is distinguished by its potato combination, its mustard dressing, and its vinegar. If you can't grill the potatoes, brush the slices with olive oil and roast them on a nonstick sheet pan in a hot oven for about 20 minutes, or until browned and tender; turn them once or twice as they cook.

Makes: 8 servings

Time: About 40 minutes

---

2 large waxy new potatoes, about 1 pound

2 large sweet potatoes, 1 pound total

¼ cup extra virgin olive oil

Salt and freshly ground black pepper

1 tablespoon grainy mustard

1 tablespoon sherry or other vinegar, or to taste

1 bunch scallions, both white and green parts, chopped

1. Start the grill. Peel the potatoes and cut them into ½-inch-thick slices, toss them with half the olive oil, and sprinkle them with salt and pepper. Grill the potatoes over direct but not-too-hot heat, turning them as they brown (it doesn't matter much whether the grill is covered, though the potatoes will cook faster if it is).

2. Remove the potato slices as they become tender (they will cook fairly quickly, in 10 to 15 minutes). When they're all done, and fairly cool, toss them with all the remaining ingredients. Taste and adjust the seasoning and serve or cover and refrigerate; bring back to room temperature before serving.

Wine: Depends on the main course

Serving: Grilled Soy-and-Ginger Boneless Leg of Lamb (Meat, Fish & Poultry, page 76) and Grilled Zucchini (page 66) for a summer barbecue

Grilled Corn

During the summer, rushing home with a bag of farmstand corn—which you can get in almost any part of the country—and cooking it on the grill is a real treat. But if you can't find locally grown, just-picked corn, you shouldn't count yourself out of the fun—new breeds of corn retain their sweetness very well. Even if you are buying your corn from the supermarket, just remember that it declines in sweetness as it ages, so it's best to cook it as soon as possible after you bring it home.

If your fire is raging hot, remove the inner silks from the corn and grill them in their husks. But if it's in the normal range, grill the shucked corn directly over the fire. Ideally, some of the kernels will brown and even char.

Makes: 4 servings

Time: 20 minutes

---

4 ears fresh corn

Melted butter (optional)

Salt and freshly ground black pepper

1. Start a grill. Shuck the corn.

2. Grill or roast the corn, turning occasionally. When some of the kernels char a bit and others are lightly browned—5 to 15 minutes, depending on the heat of the grill—the corn is done. Brush with melted butter if you like and serve with salt and pepper.

Wine: A dry wine with some fruit; Chardonnay, Viognier, even—if you can find it—Vouvray or dry Chenin Blanc

Serving: Pasta with Gorgonzola and Arugula (Pizza, Pasta & Grains, page 42), Salmon and Tomatoes Cooked in Foil (Meat, Fish & Poultry, page 10), and Simple Green Salad (page 10)

Grilled Zucchini

Zucchini cooks quickly; it is good lightly browned and still somewhat crisp or fully cooked and tender.

Makes: 8 servings

Time: 20 minutes

3 pounds zucchini, washed

¼ cup plus 2 tablespoons extra virgin olive oil

Salt and freshly ground black pepper

Chopped fresh parsley

1. Start a moderately hot grill fire. Cut the zucchini lengthwise into strips no more than ½ inch thick. Rub all the strips with ¼ cup of the olive oil and grill, turning once or twice, until nicely browned and tender, about 10 minutes.

2. Season with salt and pepper, garnish with the remaining olive oil and the parsley, and serve hot or at room temperature.

Wine: Red and rustic, like Zinfandel, Chianti, or lightly chilled Beaujolais. A cool Provençal rose wouldn't be bad either.

Serving: Grilled Soy-and-Ginger Boneless Leg of Lamb (Meat, Fish & Poultry, page 76) and Grilled Corn (page 64)

Roast New Potatoes with Rosemary

Treat new potatoes simply, using what little work you need to do to highlight their fresh and full potato flavor. I like to use heartier herbs, like rosemary, lavender, or thyme, to flavor roasted potatoes.

This preparation is classic and easy, as long as you remember it's better to overcook the potatoes than undercook them.

Makes: 4 to 6 servings

Time: 45 minutes

2 pounds new potatoes, the smaller the better, washed and dried

2 tablespoons extra virgin olive oil

1 scant tablespoon fresh rosemary leaves or 1 teaspoon dried

8 garlic cloves (optional)

Salt and freshly ground black pepper

1. Preheat the oven to 425°F. Put the potatoes in an ovenproof casserole or saucepan and toss with all the remaining ingredients. Cover and roast, shaking the pan occasionally, until the potatoes are tender, 30 to 45 minutes.

2. Uncover, stir once or twice, and serve.

Wine: A good Pinot Noir; Cabernet Sauvignon would be a close second.

Serving: Cream of Spinach Soup (Small Plates & Soups, page 54), Braised Goose with Pears or Apples (Meat, Fish & Poultry, page 56), and Herbed Green Salad with Nut Vinaigrette (page 11)

Pan-Crisped Potatoes

The late, great Pierre Franey—author of *The 60-Minute Gourmet*—showed me how to make these twenty years ago (of course, he used butter), and I have been making them weekly ever since.

Makes: 4 servings

Time: 45 minutes

2 pounds waxy red or white potatoes,
peeled and cut into ½- to 1-inch cubes

About ¼ cup olive oil

Salt and freshly ground black pepper

1 teaspoon minced garlic

1. Bring the potatoes to a boil in salted water to cover, then lower the heat and simmer until nearly tender, 10 to 15 minutes. Drain well.

2. Heat the oil over medium-high heat in a 12-inch nonstick skillet for 3 or 4 minutes. You can use more oil for crisper potatoes or less oil to cut the fat. (You can also use butter or a combination if you prefer.) Add the potatoes along with a healthy sprinkling of salt and pepper and cook, tossing and stirring from time to time (not constantly), until they are nicely browned all over, 10 to 20 minutes.

3. Add the garlic and continue to cook for 5 minutes more, stirring frequently. Taste and adjust the seasoning if necessary, then serve.

Wine: A light Pinot Noir or another fruity red, like Beaujolais

Serving: Pan-Roasted Asparagus Soup with Tarragon (Small Plates & Soups, page 62) and Broiled Salmon with Beurre Noisette (Meat, Fish & Poultry, page 8)

Fast Potato Gratin

This is a fast method for producing a delicious potato gratin. I discovered it accidentally, and it's since become a personal favorite.

Makes: 4 servings

Time: 40 minutes

---

2 pounds all-purpose potatoes, peeled and thinly sliced

Salt and freshly ground black pepper

1 teaspoon minced garlic or a grating of nutmeg (optional)

2 tablespoons unsalted butter

3 cups half-and-half or milk, or more if needed

1. Layer the potatoes in a large nonstick ovenproof skillet or roasting pan, sprinkling salt and pepper and, if you like, garlic or nutmeg between the layers. Dot with the butter, then add enough half-and-half or milk to come about three-quarters of the way to the top. Preheat the oven to 400°F.

2. Turn the heat under the potatoes to high and bring to a boil. Lower the heat to medium-high and cook for about 10 minutes, or until the level of both liquid and potatoes has subsided somewhat. Put in the oven and cook, undisturbed, until the top is nicely browned, about 10 minutes. Turn the oven heat down to 300°F and continue cooking until the potatoes are tender (a thin-bladed knife will pierce them with little or no resistance), about 10 minutes more. Serve immediately or keep warm in the oven or over very low heat for up to 30 minutes.

Wine: A decent Rioja or classified Bordeaux

Serving: Rosemary-Lemon White Bean Dip (Small Plates & Soups, page 14), Slow-Cooked Lamb with Fresh Mint Sauce (Meat, Fish & Poultry, page 82), and Green Beans with Tomatoes (page 28)

New Potatoes
with Butter and Mint

To season boiled potatoes, I like to use delicate herbs like mint, tarragon, or parsley. Mint makes a huge difference here, countering the potatoes' earthiness with its bright flavor.

Makes: 4 servings

Time: 40 minutes

About 2 pounds waxy new potatoes, the smaller the better

Salt

Several fresh mint sprigs

2 tablespoons unsalted butter, or more to taste

Minced fresh mint

1. Put the potatoes in a pot with salted water to cover; bring to a boil over high heat. Add the mint sprigs and turn the heat down to medium. Cook at a gentle boil until the potatoes are nice and tender, 20 to 40 minutes, depending on their size.

2. Drain the potatoes and return them to the pot over the lowest heat possible. Add the butter and cook, shaking the pan occasionally, until all traces of moisture have disappeared, about 5 minutes. Garnish with mint and salt as needed. Serve hot.

Wine: A crisp white would be best, like a Chablis or a comparable California Chardonnay, or even something lighter, like Pinot Grigio.

Serving: Raw Beet Salad (page 27) and Sautéed Red Snapper with Rhubarb Sauce (Meat, Fish & Poultry, page 16)

Mashed Potatoes

Mashed potatoes are easy to make. If you like them lumpy, mash them with a fork or potato masher; if you like them creamy, use a food mill or ricer. If you like them lean, omit the butter and substitute some of the potato-cooking water for the milk.

Makes: 4 servings

Time: About 40 minutes

2 pounds baking potatoes, like Idaho or russet, peeled and cut into quarters

3 tablespoons unsalted butter

¾ cup milk, gently warmed

Salt and freshly ground black pepper

1. Boil the potatoes in salted water to cover until soft, about 30 minutes.

2. When the potatoes are done, drain them, then mash them well or put them through a food mill. Return them to the pot over very low heat and stir in the butter and—gradually—the milk, beating with a wooden spoon until smooth and creamy. Season with salt and pepper. Serve immediately, keep warm, or reheat in a microwave.

Wine: Depends on the main dish

Serving: This classic side pairs well with most proteins and greens.

Skewered Crisp Shiitakes with Garlic

One of the great advances of the modern supermarket was the appearance of fresh shiitake mushrooms on a regular basis.

Makes: 20 skewers, enough for 8 to 10

Time: About 1 hour

40 shiitake caps, about 1 pound (stems should be reserved for stock or discarded)

⅓ cup extra virgin olive oil

1 tablespoon chopped garlic

Salt and freshly ground black pepper

1. Preheat the oven to 450°F. Put the shiitakes in one layer in a roasting pan and toss with the olive oil. Roast for about 20 minutes, until the shiitakes have begun to shrink. Stir in the garlic, salt, and pepper and return to the oven, tossing and turning occasionally, until the shiitakes are crisp, another 20 minutes or so.

2. Cool slightly, then skewer the mushrooms on toothpicks. Serve warm.

Wine: If serving at a cocktail party, Champagne or cocktails, or both white and red wines

Serving: Rosemary-Lemon White Bean Dip (Small Plates & Soups, page 14), and Prosciutto, Fig, and Parmesan Rolls (Small Plates & Soups, page 8) for a cocktail party

Porcini-Scented "Wild" Mushroom Sauté

How to get great flavor out of ordinary white mushrooms? Add a handful of dried porcini. You will not believe the difference.

Makes: 4 servings

Time: 30 minutes

½ cup dried porcini

¼ cup extra virgin olive oil

1 pound button mushrooms, trimmed and sliced

Salt and freshly ground black pepper

1 teaspoon minced garlic

2 tablespoons minced fresh parsley

1. Pour boiling water over the porcini to reconstitute; let them sit for about 10 minutes or until tender, then drain and trim off any hard spots.

2. Put the olive oil in a large skillet over high heat; a minute later, add the porcini and button mushrooms, along with a big pinch of salt and some pepper, and cook, stirring occasionally, until the mushrooms give off most of their liquid and begin to brown, about 10 minutes. Turn the heat to medium-low and add the garlic. Continue to cook for a few more minutes, until the mixture is tender and glossy. Taste and adjust the seasoning, stir in the parsley, and serve hot or warm.

Wine: Chianti or any other fruity but gutsy red, like Zinfandel or a Côtes du Rhône

Serving: Pasta with Fast Sausage Ragù (Pizza, Pasta & Grains, page 50), Chicken with Pancetta and Balsamic Vinegar (Meat, Fish & Poultry, page 48), and 60-Minute Bread (Pizza, Pasta & Grains, page 72)

Quick Scallion Pancakes

These are simpler than traditional scallion pancakes, which are made from a breadlike dough, and they taste more like scallions, because the "liquid" is scallion puree. The flavor is great, the preparation time is cut to about twenty minutes, and the texture is that of a vegetable fritter.

Because the batter is so delicate, it's better to make these as individual pancakes, which are easy to turn, than as one big cake.

I use peanut oil for this recipe, but that's only because I associate it with soy sauce. If you omit the soy you can use any vegetable oil you like, even good olive oil.

Makes: 4 servings

Time: About 30 minutes

---

4 bunches of scallions (about 1 pound)

1 egg

1 teaspoon soy sauce

½ cup flour

Freshly ground black pepper

Peanut, corn, or olive oil as needed

1. Bring a pot of salted water to a boil while you trim the scallions. Roughly chop about three-quarters of them and mince the remainder.

2. Add the larger portion of scallions to the water and cook for about 5 minutes, or until tender. Drain, reserving about ½ cup of the cooking liquid. Puree the cooked scallions in a blender, adding just enough of the cooking liquid to allow the machine to do its work.

3. Mix the puree with the egg and soy sauce, then gently stir in the flour until blended; add pepper and the reserved minced scallions. Film a nonstick or well-seasoned skillet with oil and turn the heat to medium-high. Drop the batter by the tablespoon or ¼ cup and cook the pancakes for about 2 minutes per side, until lightly browned. If necessary, the pancakes can be kept warm in a 200°F oven for about 30 minutes.

Variations

The same method can be used to make pancakes with many members of the onion family, especially shallots and spring onions (which look like scallions on steroids). There are also some quick additions to the batter to vary the pancakes:

» Toasted sesame seeds, about 1 tablespoon

» Roughly chopped peanuts, about 2 tablespoons

» Minced chives, added along with the uncooked scallions, about ¼ cup

» Cayenne to taste

» Minced fresh ginger, a tablespoon or so

Wine: Beer would be best here.

Serving: Asian-Style Cucumber Soup (Small Plates & Soups, page 46) and Fresh Chinese Noodles with Brown Sauce (Pizza, Pasta & Grains, page 64)

Watermelon, Thai Style

A frequently seen snack in Bangkok and elsewhere in Southeast Asia.

Makes: 8 servings

Time: 10 minutes

Eight 1-inch-thick wedges of watermelon

Salt, to pass at the table

Finely ground dried chiles, to pass at the table

Lime wedges, to pass at the table

Put the watermelon on plates and pass the remaining ingredients, allowing guests to season the melon to taste.

Wine: Beer would be best.

Serving: For an Asian-inspired meal, serve with Stir-Fried Coconut Noodles (Pizza, Pasta & Grains, page 56) and Herbed Green Salad with Soy Vinaigrette (page 12).

Cool Cooked Greens with Lemon

The only precaution here is not to overcook. You want the greens to be just short of perfectly cooked when you remove them from the boiling water and run under cold water.

Makes: 4 servings

Time: 20 minutes

---

2 pounds dark leafy greens, like collards, kale, or spinach

Several tablespoons extra virgin olive oil

Salt and freshly ground black pepper

2 lemons, cut in half

1. Bring a large pot of water to a boil and salt it. Trim the greens of any stems thicker than ¼ inch; discard them. Wash the greens well.

2. Simmer the greens until tender, just a minute or two for spinach, up to 10 minutes or even longer for older, tougher greens. Drain them well and cool them quickly by running them under cold water.

3. Squeeze the greens dry and chop them. (You may prepare the dish in advance up to this point; cover and refrigerate for up to a day, then bring to room temperature before proceeding.) Sprinkle with olive oil, salt, and pepper, and serve with lemon halves.

Variations

There's little you cannot do with precooked greens, but here are some good ideas:

» Sprinkle the cooked greens with toasted slivered nuts, bread crumbs, or sesame seeds.

» Add a teaspoon or so of garlic to the butter and/or oil as it is cooking; or use a tablespoon or two of minced shallot, onion, or scallion.

(continued)

» Add a tablespoon or more of soy sauce to the finished greens, with or without the lemon.

» Substitute lime juice or vinegar for the lemon juice. Or use any vinaigrette as a dressing.

Wine: White, cool, and simple: a Graves, Pinot Blanc, Pinot Gris, Pinot Grigio, or a blend from the south of France

Serving: Herbed Farmer, Goat, or Cream Cheese (Small Plates & Soups, page 11), Broiled Salmon with Beurre Noisette (Meat, Fish & Poultry, page 8), and 60-Minute Bread (Pizza, Pasta & Grains, page 72)

Marinated Olives

The ease with which this dish can be thrown together and the range of meals it happily accompanies (menus with European, Middle Eastern, or Northern African accents are game, as are good old American cookouts) guarantee that it makes regular and frequent appearances on my dinner table.

An assortment of olives is far preferable to just one kind. Try, for example, some oil cured, some big fat green Sicilians, and some kalamatas—just that simple combination will look bright and pretty. If you can lay your hands on more varieties, so much the better.

Makes: 4 servings

Time: 1 hour, largely unattended

2 cups assorted olives

4 garlic cloves, peeled and lightly crushed

2 tablespoons extra virgin olive oil

1 teaspoon fresh rosemary leaves

1 small lemon, cut in half and segmented like a grapefruit

1. Toss all the ingredients together in a bowl. Marinate for an hour or longer at room temperature.

2. After the first day, refrigerate, then remove from the refrigerator an hour or two before serving. These will keep for weeks.

Wine: Should be determined by the main course

Serving: These are a great appetizer for a dinner party.

Cauliflower with Garlic and Anchovy

Buy snow-white cauliflower with no brown spots; use broccoli or one of the hybrids (broccoflower, Romanesco broccoli, and so on) if the cauliflower does not look good. And though it is a full-flavored dish, remember that cooking will mellow the assertive flavors of the anchovies and garlic, so don't skimp on either. This dish is just as good warm as it is hot.

Makes: 4 servings

Time: About 30 minutes

---

1 large head of cauliflower (at least 2 pounds), trimmed and cut or broken into florets

Salt

¼ cup plus 2 tablespoons extra virgin olive oil

5 to 10 anchovy fillets, to taste, chopped

1 tablespoon minced garlic

1 teaspoon hot red pepper flakes, or to taste (optional)

Minced fresh parsley

1. Put the cauliflower in a steamer above an inch or two of boiling salted water. Cover and cook until it is just tender, about 10 minutes, then plunge into a bowl of ice water to stop the cooking.

2. Combine the oil, anchovies, garlic, and hot pepper if you're using it in a large deep skillet and turn the heat to medium-low. Cook, stirring occasionally, until the anchovies begin to break up and the garlic begins to color, about 5 minutes.

3. Add the cauliflower and raise the heat to medium-high. Continue to cook, stirring, for about 5 minutes more, until the cauliflower is coated with oil and heated through. Garnish with parsley and serve hot or at room temperature.

Wine: Dark and red: Something made with the Nebbiolo grape (like Barolo or Barbaresco) would be ideal.

Serving: Pasta with Dark Red Duck Sauce (Pizza, Pasta & Grains, page 52) and 60-Minute Bread (Pizza, Pasta & Grains, page 72)

Index

About the Author

Mark Bittman created and wrote the weekly *New York Times* column "The Minimalist," which ran for thirteen years. He currently covers food policy and all topics related to eating in a weekly op-ed column for the *New York Times*, and is the lead writer for the *Eat* column in the Sunday *New York Times Magazine*.

Bittman has written more than a dozen cookbooks, including *The Minimalist Cooks at Home*, *The Minimalist Cooks Dinner*, *The Minimalist Entertains*, as well as the popular family of kitchen standards *How to Cook Everything*, *How to Cook Everything Vegetarian*, and *How to Cook Everything The Basics*. Bittman explores global cuisines in *The Best Recipes in the World*, an inspired collection of recipes culled from his international travels. With Jean-Georges Vongerichten, he coauthored *Jean-Georges* (winner of a James Beard Award) and *Simple to Spectacular*. And his bestselling *Food Matters* and *Food Matters Cookbook* offer simple ways to improve your diet and the health of the planet.

As a longtime feature on commercial and public television, Bittman has hosted three award-winning cooking series on PBS, is often invited to share his viewpoints on news and magazine programs, and appears regularly on the *Today* show. He also records a weekly web video for the magazine, revisiting recipes from the beloved Minimalist column. For more information, visit www.markbittman.com.

Notes

The Mini Minimalist
Small Plates & Soups

Mark Bittman
The Mini Minimalist

Small Plates & Soups

Clarkson Potter/Publishers
New York

Based on the following books
by Mark Bittman: *The Minimalist
Cooks at Home,* copyright
© 2000 by Mark Bittman;
The Minimalist Cooks Dinner,
copyright © 2001 by Mark
Bittman; and *The Minimalist
Entertains,* copyright © 2003
by Mark Bittman.

—————————————————————

Printed in China

Written by Mark Bittman

Design by Jan Derevjanik

Contents

Small Plates

Prosciutto, Fig, and Parmesan Rolls

A simple, stand-up, make-in-advance starter.

Makes: About 20 rolls, enough for 8 people

Time: 20 minutes

½ pound prosciutto, sliced very thin

About ¼ pound Parmesan, sliced wafer-thin

8 to 10 dried figs, stemmed and cut into about 3 strips each

Truffle or extra virgin olive oil

1. Cut each piece of prosciutto in half the long way; on each piece, put a slice of Parmesan and a strip of fig. Roll up the long way, pressing so that the meat sticks to itself. Cover with plastic wrap if not serving right away.

2. Serve within 2 hours, drizzling with truffle oil just before serving.

Wine: Red, for sure, preferably something rich and wonderful; a classified Bordeaux or a good California Cabernet

Serving: Serve as an appetizer for a simple but grand meal.

Figs Stuffed with Goat Cheese

Fall is the time for fresh figs, which people who live in Mediterranean climates (this includes many Californians) take for granted but are a real treat for the rest of us.

Makes: 8 servings

Time: 15 minutes

---

4 to 6 ounces soft, fresh goat cheese

1 tablespoon good balsamic vinegar

16 fresh figs, washed and drained

1. Use your fingers to roll the goat cheese into 32 small balls, each ½ inch or less in diameter. Place them on a plate and drizzle with the vinegar. Shake the plate gently to coat the cheese balls evenly.

2. Cut the figs in half and press a cheese ball into the center of each half. As the figs are stuffed, return them, stuffed side up, to the plate where the cheese was marinating. Serve within an hour.

Wine: A fruity red; perhaps a Côtes du Rhône blend, or a Chianti Classico

Serving: Could be served as an appetizer for a Mediterranean dinner

Fig Relish

While the best way to eat figs is out of hand—few fruits are as delicious when ripe—there are rewarding ways to use them in recipes; this fig relish is one of them. It is especially brilliant on grilled swordfish or tuna, but nearly as good with grilled or broiled chicken (especially dark meat), pork, lamb, or beef. Note that all of these foods contain some fat; because the relish is so lean, combining it with non-fatty meats or fish—such as boneless chicken or flounder—produces a dish that seems to lack substance.

Makes: 4 servings

Time: 10 minutes

½ pound ripe fresh figs

1 tablespoon minced drained capers

Zest of 1 lemon, minced

Juice of 1 lemon

2 tablespoons extra virgin olive oil

Salt and freshly ground black pepper

2 tablespoons chopped fresh parsley

2 tablespoons chopped fresh basil (optional)

Lemon wedges

Gently rinse and stem the figs; chop them into about ¼-inch pieces, being sure to catch all of their juices. Toss in a bowl with the capers, lemon zest and juice, olive oil, and salt and pepper to taste. Just before serving (you can wait up to 2 hours), add the herbs, then taste and adjust the seasonings. Serve with lemon wedges.

Wine: It depends on the food you're serving it with, but most likely you'll be wanting a red with substance.

Serving: The fig relish is great with grilled tuna or swordfish, and good with grilled or broiled chicken (especially dark meat), pork, lamb, beef.

Herbed Farmer, Goat, or Cream Cheese

A wonderful showcase for any herb, but the thyme-garlic combo is most familiar and probably the most broadly appealing.

Makes: 8 servings

Time: 10 minutes, plus about 30 minutes to rest

1 pound cold farmer cheese, fresh goat cheese, or cream cheese

½ cup sour cream

1 tablespoon fresh thyme leaves, or more to taste

½ garlic clove, or more if you like

Salt and freshly ground black pepper

1. Combine all the ingredients in a food processor and blend until smooth. (Alternatively, mince the garlic and mash all the ingredients with a potato masher or fork until fairly smooth, then beat for a few moments with a wire whisk.) Taste and adjust the seasoning as necessary.

2. Scrape into a bowl and refrigerate until stiffened. Serve with crackers, lightly toasted pita, and/or raw vegetable sticks.

Wine: Pinot Blanc, Pinot Gris, Pinot Grigio, or a blend from the south of France

Serving: Use as a dip for breadsticks, pita or other bread, or raw vegetables.

Parmesan Cups
with Orzo Risotto

A couple of years ago, on a trip to central Italy—where true Parmigiano-Reggiano is made—I learned yet another use for the world's most important cheese. A cook in a trattoria was taking handfuls of the grated stuff, sprinkling them in a skillet, and forming melted cheese pancakes. While they were still warm, he draped them over the back of a cup, to form crisp, edible, single-ingredient containers. He filled these with a mixture of zucchini, eggplant, and tomatoes and sent them out as a first course.

I found the idea intriguing, but not all that easy to duplicate at home, where my skillet seemed always too hot or too cool, the pancakes too thick or too thin. But, thanks to the miracle of the nonstick surface, just put four rounds of grated cheese on a baking sheet and, five minutes later, they're done.

Makes: 4 servings

Time: 30 minutes

2 cups good-quality chicken or other stock

1 cup orzo (rice-shaped pasta)

1 cup freshly grated Parmigiano-Reggiano cheese, about ¼ pound

Salt and freshly ground black pepper

½ cup minced fresh parsley

1. Preheat the oven to 350°F

2. Bring the stock to a boil in a 6- to 8-cup saucepan; stir in the orzo, cover, and turn the heat to medium-low. Set a timer for 15 minutes.

3. Use a ¼-cup measure to make 4 rounds of Parmigiano-Reggiano on a nonstick baking sheet. Smooth the rounds into thin pancakes, 5 or 6 inches across; the thickness need not be perfectly uniform. Put the baking sheet in the oven.

4. The Parmigiano-Reggiano rounds are done when the centers darken slightly and the edges begin to brown, 5 to 6 minutes. Remove the baking sheet from the oven and let it stand for about a minute, then carefully lift each of the rounds and drape it over the bottom of a narrow cup or glass to form a cup shape. Let dry for about 5 minutes.

5. The orzo is done when it is tender and all the liquid has been absorbed. Season it with pepper and very little salt, then stir in the parsley. Spoon a portion of orzo into each of the Parmigiano-Reggiano cups and serve.

Wine: You can break out a good red here, like Cabernet or Pinot Noir.

Serving: An elegant but filling starter like this should be followed by something simple, perhaps broiled or grilled fish.

Rosemary-Lemon White Bean Dip

This wonderful dip originally came to me from Lidia Bastianich, one of the great Italian educators, chefs, and TV personalities. It has more life than most dips but does without the harshness of raw garlic usually associated with Middle Eastern hummus or Southwestern purees. Still, it's pretty simple, with the not-exactly-exotic "mystery" ingredient of grated lemon zest, which is quite substantial in both quantity and size of the pieces.

Makes: 4 servings

Time: 10 minutes (with precooked or canned beans)

2 cups cooked cannellini or other white beans, drained but quite moist

2 garlic cloves, peeled

Salt and freshly ground black pepper

¼ cup extra virgin olive oil

1 tablespoon minced fresh rosemary

Grated zest of 1 lemon

1. Put the beans in a food processor with the garlic and a healthy pinch of salt. Turn the machine on and add half the olive oil in a steady stream through the feed tube; process until the mixture is smooth.

2. Put the mixture in a bowl and use a wooden spoon to beat in the rosemary, lemon zest, and remaining olive oil. Taste and add salt and pepper as needed. Use immediately or refrigerate for up to 3 days.

Wine: Will depend on the center-of-the-plate food.

Serving: Use the puree as a dip for breadsticks, pita or other bread, or raw vegetables.

Real Onion Sour Cream Dip

As you can imagine, substituting freshly cooked crisp onions makes a far better dip than using dried onion soup mix.

Makes: About 1 cup, enough for 8 servings

Time: 15 minutes active, plus time to chill

⅓ cup neutral oil, such as grape seed or vegetable

1 medium onion, minced, about ½ cup

Pinch of salt

¼ teaspoon sugar

1 cup sour cream

1. Place the oil in an 8-inch skillet and turn the heat to medium-high. When it's hot, a minute or two later, add the onion, salt, and sugar. Cook, shaking the pan occasionally, until the onion browns, about 10 minutes.

2. Pour the onion and oil into a fine strainer; reserve the oil for another use (refrigerate it in the meantime). Stir the onion into the sour cream; cover and refrigerate for 24 hours or so if time allows.

Wine: Will depend on the center-of-the-plate food.

Serving: Serve with potato chips or cut-up vegetables.

Grilled Eggplant Dip

Grilling is an important part of this dish, as it gives the eggplant a smoky flavor that's hard to come by otherwise.

Makes: 8 servings

Time: About 1 hour

2 medium or 4 small eggplant, about 1 pound total

¼ cup fresh lemon juice

¼ cup extra virgin olive oil

½ teaspoon minced garlic, or to taste

Salt and freshly ground black pepper

Minced fresh parsley leaves

1. Start a charcoal, wood, or gas grill; pierce the eggplant in several places with a thin-bladed knife or skewer. Grill, turning occasionally, until the eggplant collapses and the skin blackens, 15 to 30 minutes depending on size. Remove and cool.

2. When the eggplant is cool enough to handle, part the skin (if it hasn't split on its own), scoop out the flesh, and mince it finely. Mix it with the lemon juice, oil, garlic, salt, and pepper. Taste and adjust the seasonings, then garnish with the parsley.

Wine: Cold rosé, or something red and rough, or a light wine like Beaujolais, lightly chilled

Serving: Serve as an appetizer with grilled flatbreads.

Canapés with Piquillo Peppers and Anchovies

Piquillo peppers are wood-roasted peppers from Spain, sold in cans or jars. If you cannot find them, substitute homemade roasted peppers or canned "pimientos."

Makes: 4 servings

Time: 20 minutes

8 thick slices (roughly ¾ inch) French or Italian bread, cut in half

1 teaspoon minced garlic

8 piquillo peppers, cut in half, or 4 or 5 roasted peppers (Vegetables, page 58)

16 oil-packed anchovies

Extra virgin olive oil

Lightly toast the bread. Top each piece with a tiny bit of garlic, then layer with a piece of piquillo and an anchovy. Drizzle with a little anchovy oil and/or olive oil. Serve within an hour.

Wine: Côtes du Rhône blend or a Chianti Classico

Serving: Serve as a starter before Pasta alla Gricia (Pizza, Pasta & Grains, page 44).

Dried Mushroom Puree

It isn't often that you can make a condiment with a single dried ingredient, but since dried mushrooms have become widely available, that occurrence has become more common. If you simmer dried mushrooms until tender, then toss them in a blender with their cooking liquid, you get a thick puree, potent and delicious, something you can use wherever you'd use salsa or even ketchup.

You can use any dried mushrooms for this condiment, from the extremely inexpensive shiitakes (also called black mushrooms) sold at Asian markets to the prince of dried mushrooms, the porcini. Smoky porcini (usually imported from Chile or Poland) are really good here.

The result is very much like the classic duxelles, in which fresh mushrooms and their scraps are cooked only until their essence remains. But this procedure requires almost no preparation: no cleaning, no chopping, and hardly any cooking, because the mushrooms have already been dried and there is no need to cook out their water.

Makes: 4 servings

Time: 20 minutes

---

1 ounce dried porcini, about ½ cup loosely packed

Salt and freshly ground black pepper

1. Combine the mushrooms with 2½ cups of water in a 4- or 6-cup saucepan and turn the heat to medium-high. Bring to a boil, then adjust the heat so the mixture simmers gently. Cook until the mushrooms are tender, about 15 minutes.

2. Remove the mushrooms with a slotted spoon and put in a blender. Strain the liquid through a sieve lined with a paper towel or a couple of layers of cheesecloth; there will be about 1 cup. Add most of the liquid to the mushrooms and puree, adding the remaining liquid if necessary to allow the machine to do its work.

3. Season to taste with salt and pepper and serve or cover and refrigerate for up to a couple of days.

Wine: Most likely a red, to be determined by the center-of-the plate food

Serving: Stir the puree into risotto or other grain preparations (be sure to use any of the leftover mushroom-cooking liquid in cooking the grain); include it in omelets or in pizzas; thin it with butter or olive oil to make a sauce for meat or fish; or simply use it as you would ketchup.

Chawan-Mushi

Chawan-mushi is an egg custard flavored with stock and soy and laced with a number of tasty tidbits. In Tokyo, I had a bowl that contained tiny amounts of *myoga* (a potent member of the onion family), shrimp, chicken, and ginkgo nut. None of these is essential, and you can substitute for any or all of them, as I do in the recipe below.

Makes: 8 servings

Time: 30 minutes

24 leaves watercress

8 sea scallops, each cut into 4 pieces

4 shallots, chopped

Salt and freshly ground black pepper

8 eggs

3 cups chicken or beef stock or dashi

2 tablespoons soy sauce

1. Put one-eighth of the watercress, scallops, and shallots in each of eight 6-ounce ramekins and sprinkle with salt and pepper. Beat the eggs lightly and combine with the stock and soy.

2. Put the ramekins in a deep baking pan or skillet and fill them with the egg mixture. Add boiling water about halfway up the height of the ramekins and turn the heat to high. When the water returns to the boil, turn the heat to low, and cover tightly.

3. Simmer for 15 minutes, then check. The custards are done when they have set and are no longer watery, but are still quite jiggly. Remove them from the water immediately and serve hot, warm, or at room temperature.

Wine: Dry sake or a not-perfectly-dry Riesling

Serving: Serve with white or brown rice for a simple Japanese meal.

Gravlax

The intense orange color, meltingly tender texture, and wonderful flavor of gravlax give it an allure shared by few fish preparations— not bad for a dish whose name means "buried salmon" in Swedish. The curing process intensifies the color, tenderizes the texture, and enhances the flavor. Although most chefs jazz up gravlax with sauces and side dishes, it is brilliant on its own, or with just a few drops of lemon or mild vinegar. And the rankest kitchen novice can make it at home.

Makes: At least 12 servings

Time: At least 24 hours, largely unattended

1 cup salt

2 cups sugar

1 bunch dill, stems and all, chopped

One 2- to 3-pound fillet of salmon, pin bones removed

1. Mix together the salt, sugar, and dill. Place the salmon, skin side down, on a large sheet of plastic wrap. Cover the flesh side of the salmon with the salt mixture, making sure to coat it completely (there will be lots of salt mix; just pile it on there).

2. Wrap the fish well. If the air temperature is below 70 degrees and it is not too inconvenient, let it rest outside the refrigerator for about 6 hours, then refrigerate for 18 to 24 hours more. Otherwise, refrigerate immediately for about 36 hours.

3. Unwrap the salmon and rinse off the cure. Dry, then slice on the bias. Serve plain or with lemon wedges, crème fraîche, sour cream, or a light vinaigrette.

Wine: Champagne or a good white, preferably Burgundy

Serving: This is a starter, to be served with bread.

Minty Broiled Shrimp Salad

When I was making this salad one time, it rained so hard I was forced to resort to the broiler. It was then I remembered why broiled shrimp are so desirable: You get to savor the delicious juices, the essences, produced by the shrimp themselves.

This newfound liquid and the time of year cried for a bed of greens. Not wanting to completely overwhelm delicately flavored greens with the powerfully spiced shrimp, I used a mixture of arugula, lettuce, and a high proportion of mint, dressed with olive oil and lemon juice. The result is a nice, juicy, big, flavorful—and easy—salad.

Makes: 4 servings

Time: 20 to 30 minutes

2 pounds shrimp in the 15-to-30-per-pound range, peeled (and deveined if you like)

1 teaspoon minced garlic, or to taste

1 teaspoon salt

½ teaspoon cayenne pepper, or to taste

1 teaspoon paprika

¼ cup olive oil

2 tablespoons plus 2 teaspoons fresh lemon juice

30 to 40 mint leaves

6 cups arugula and/or other greens

1. Preheat the broiler, and adjust the rack so that it is as close to the heat source as possible. Place a large ovenproof skillet or thick-bottomed roasting pan on the stove over low heat.

2. Combine the shrimp with the garlic, salt, cayenne, paprika, half the olive oil, and the 2 teaspoons lemon juice; stir to blend. Turn the heat under the skillet to high. When the skillet smokes, toss in the shrimp. Shake the pan once or twice to distribute them evenly, then immediately place the skillet in the broiler.

3. Mince about one-third of the mint. Tear the remaining leaves and toss them with the arugula. Stir the remaining olive oil and lemon juice together in a bowl.

4. The shrimp are done when opaque; this will take only 3 or 4 minutes. Use a slotted spoon to transfer the shrimp to a plate; it's fine if they cool for a moment. Add the shrimp juices to the olive oil–lemon juice mixture and stir. Dress the greens with this mixture and toss (if the greens seem dry, add a little more olive oil, lemon juice, or both). Place the greens on a platter and arrange the shrimp on top of or around them; garnish the shrimp with the minced mint.

Wine: Any fresh, crisp, and inexpensive white, like Pinot Grigio or Muscadet

Serving: Can be served in smaller portions as a starter, or large portions with a bit of crusty bread for a whole-meal dish

Shrimp with Better Cocktail Sauce

This is a rich cocktail sauce, laced with butter but made spicy with vinegar and horseradish—make it as hot as you like, and serve it warm or cold.

Makes: 8 servings

Time: 30 minutes

3 pounds large shrimp, peeled

1 cup ketchup

1 tablespoon vinegar

3 tablespoons unsalted butter

2 tablespoons prepared horseradish, or to taste

1. Put the shrimp in a saucepan with water to cover. Turn the heat to high and bring to a boil. Cover the pan, remove from the heat, and let sit for 10 minutes. Drain and chill (you can run the shrimp under cold water if you're in a hurry).

2. Combine the ketchup, vinegar, and butter in a small saucepan and cook over medium-low heat, stirring occasionally, until the butter melts. (At this point, you can keep the sauce warm for an hour— but turn the heat as low as possible.) Add the horseradish.

Wine: Champagne, cocktails, or both white and red wines

Serving: Serve as an appetizer for a cocktail party with Prosciutto, Fig, and Parmesan Rolls (page 8), Rosemary-Lemon White Bean Dip (page 14), and Miso-Broiled Scallops (page 29).

Soy-Dipped Shrimp

Many people will find this their idea of paradise: simply grilled shrimp in a strong-flavored soy dipping sauce.

Makes: 8 servings

Time: 40 minutes

2 tablespoons medium-hot paprika

¼ cup peanut oil

Salt and freshly ground black pepper

3 pounds large shrimp, peeled

1 cup good soy sauce

1 tablespoon minced garlic

1 tablespoon minced peeled fresh ginger

¼ cup fresh lemon juice

¼ teaspoon cayenne, or to taste

1. Start a grill fire. Mix the paprika, peanut oil, salt, and pepper, and rub all over the shrimp. When the fire is moderately hot, grill the shrimp, turning once, until done, about 5 minutes. Meanwhile, mix the soy sauce with the garlic, ginger, lemon juice, and cayenne; taste and adjust the seasoning as necessary.

2. Serve the shrimp hot, with the soy dipping sauce.

Wine: Beer

Serving: Serve as a starter, ideal before grilled meat and a salad.

Scallop Seviche

This is a true seviche, one in which the scallops are "cooked" by the acidity of the citrus.

Makes: 8 servings

Time: 30 minutes

1 pound perfectly fresh sea scallops, cut into ¼-inch dice

3 tablespoons minced bell pepper, preferably a combination of red, yellow, and green

1 teaspoon minced lemon zest

1 tablespoon fresh orange juice

1 tablespoon fresh lemon juice

Salt

Cayenne to taste

2 tablespoons minced fresh cilantro (optional)

1. Toss together all the ingredients, except the cilantro, and let sit at room temperature for 15 minutes.

2. Taste, adjust the seasoning, and serve, garnished with the cilantro, if you like.

Wine: A light, simple white, like Pinot Grigio

Serving: Serve as an appetizer for a sit-down dinner of Slow Cooked Duck Legs with Olives (Meat, Fish & Poultry, page 54) and Roasted Asparagus with Parmesan (Vegetables, page 45).

Miso-Broiled Scallops

An appetizer that brilliantly displays the complexity of miso.

Makes: 8 servings

Time: 20 minutes active

¾ cup miso

3 tablespoons mirin, fruity white wine, or dry white wine

1 cup minced onion

Salt and cayenne

2 pounds sea scallops

Juice of 1 lime

1. Preheat a broiler or grill, setting the rack as close as possible to the heat source. Put the miso in a bowl, add the mirin, and whisk until smooth. Stir in the onion, a little bit of salt, and a pinch of cayenne. Add the scallops and let them marinate while the broiler or grill preheats; or refrigerate for up to a day.

2. Broil until lightly browned, without turning, 2 to 3 minutes, or grill, turning once after a minute or two. Sprinkle with the lime juice and serve with toothpicks.

Wine: Champagne, cocktails, or both white and red wines

Serving: Serve as an appetizer for a cocktail party with Prosciutto, Fig, and Parmesan Rolls (page 8), Rosemary-Lemon White Bean Dip (page 14), and Shrimp with Better Cocktail Sauce (page 26).

Stuffed Scallops

The sea scallop is one of the most perfect of nature's convenience foods—almost nothing cooks faster. This is especially true if you opt to heat the mollusk until it remains rare in the center, as do most scallop admirers. (Shuckers separate the scallop's meat from its guts soon after capture, which makes scallops the safest shellfish to eat undercooked or even raw.)

Sea scallops are also large enough to stuff, not with bread crumbs or other fish, as is common with clams or lobsters, but with herbs, garlic, and other flavorings. As long as a scallop is a good inch across and roughly three-quarters of an inch thick, you can make an equatorial slit in it and fill it with any number of stuffings.

Makes: 4 servings

Time: 30 minutes

20 large fresh basil leaves

1 small garlic clove, peeled

½ teaspoon coarse salt

¼ teaspoon freshly ground black pepper

3 tablespoons extra virgin olive oil

1¼ to 1½ pounds large sea scallops of fairly uniform size

1. Mince the basil, garlic, salt and pepper together until very fine, almost a puree (use a small food processor if you like). Mix in a small bowl with 1 tablespoon of the olive oil to produce a thick paste.

2. Cut most but not all of the way through the equator of each scallop, then smear a bit of the basil mixture on the exposed center; close the scallop.

3. Place a large nonstick skillet over high heat for a minute; add the remaining oil, then the scallops, one at a time. As each scallop browns—it should take no longer than 1 or 2 minutes—turn it and brown the other side. Serve hot, drizzled with pan juices.

Wine: A not-too-subtle red, like Chianti, Zinfandel, or something from the south of France

Serving: Nice before a dish like Spaghetti with Fresh Tomato Sauce (Pizza, Pasta & Grains, page 26), served with bread and salad.

Mussels, Asian Style

Most steamed mussel preparations contain parsley, garlic, and white wine, with the occasional addition of tomatoes and herbs. There are, however, other directions in which you can prepare mussels, and they're no more effort than the familiar ones.

Generally, there are two easy changes to make: First, use distinctive Asian seasonings such as ginger, soy, or curry powder. And second, omit the cooking liquid. By relying only on the mussels' natural juices, you can add fewer seasonings (and less of each) and still produce a flavorful sauce that is less watery than most.

Makes: 4 servings

Time: 30 minutes

2 tablespoons peanut or canola oil

¼ cup roughly chopped scallions

1 tablespoon roughly chopped peeled fresh ginger

2 cloves garlic, peeled and lightly smashed

4 pounds mussels, well washed

1 tablespoon soy sauce

1. Put the oil in a saucepan large enough to hold all the mussels and turn the heat to medium. A minute later, add the scallions, ginger, and garlic and cook, stirring occasionally, for about 1 minute.

2. Add the mussels, turn the heat to high, and cover the pot. Cook, shaking the pot occasionally, until they all (or nearly all) open, about 10 minutes. Turn off the heat.

3. Scoop the mussels into a serving bowl. Add the soy sauce to the liquid, then pass it through a fine strainer (or a coarse one lined with cheesecloth). Pour the liquid over the mussels and serve.

Wine: Champagne, beer, or Gewürztraminer

Serving: If you're making these as part of a light meal, serve with a salad. If you're using them as a starter, follow with Vietnamese-Style Pork (Meat, Fish & Poultry, page 85) and rice.

Fennel-Steamed Mussels, Provence Style

In a café in southern France more than twenty years ago, I sat in a bistro and timidly prepared to order salade Niçoise. Just then, a huge bowl of steaming, powerfully fragrant mussels was delivered to a man sitting at the table next to me, and I impulsively changed my order. The hot mussels were essentially tossed with fennel and fennel seeds, which I could see, but the licorice bouquet and indeed flavor were far stronger than that combination alone could provide. Later, I realized that there was a secret ingredient: anise liqueur, either Pernod or Ricard. The combination is an alluring one.

Makes: 4 servings

Time: 20 to 30 minutes

2 tablespoons extra virgin olive oil

4 garlic cloves, smashed and peeled

1 fennel bulb, about 1 pound, trimmed and thinly sliced

2 tablespoons fennel seeds

¼ cup Pernod or Ricard (or 4 pieces star anise)

1 cup chopped tomatoes (canned are fine; drain them first), optional

1 sprig tarragon (optional)

4 pounds mussels, well washed

1. Pour the oil into a large pot, turn the heat to medium, and heat for a minute. Add the garlic, fennel, fennel seeds, liqueur, tomatoes, and tarragon, if you like. Bring to a boil, cook for about a minute, add the mussels, cover the pot, and turn the heat to high.

2. Cook, shaking the pot occasionally, until the mussels open, about 10 minutes. Use a slotted spoon to transfer the mussels and fennel to a serving bowl, then strain any liquid over them and serve.

Wine: White, crisp, and cold—Muscadet, an inexpensive Italian white, or a good Sauvignon Blanc

Serving: Serve with 60-Minute Bread (Pizza, Pasta & Grains, page 72) or good store-bought bread and Simple Green Salad (Vegetables, page 10).

Crabby Crab Cakes

Crab has the best texture and among the best flavors of all the crustaceans, and the best crab cakes are those that showcase the crab most fully. So getting the most out of crab cakes often means putting the least into them. When you start loading crab cakes up with white bread, corn, curry, and complicated sauces, you might be making them different, but you're not making them better. I usually serve my crab cakes with nothing more than lemon wedges, but tartar sauce and aïoli are both excellent choices if you choose to make a condiment.

Makes: 4 servings

Time: 1 hour, largely unattended

---

1 pound fresh lump crabmeat

1 egg

1 tablespoon Dijon mustard (optional)

Salt and freshly ground black pepper

2 tablespoons flour, plus more for dredging

¼ cup extra virgin olive oil or neutral oil, like corn or grapeseed

Lemon wedges

1. Gently combine the crab, egg, mustard if you're using it, salt and pepper to taste, and 2 tablespoons flour. Cover and put in the freezer for 5 minutes. Shape the mixture into 4 patties. Line a plate with plastic wrap and put the crab cakes on it. Cover with more plastic wrap and refrigerate for about 30 minutes (or up to a day if you like) or freeze for 15 minutes.

2. Put the flour for dredging in a bowl. Put the oil in a 12-inch skillet over medium heat. When the oil is hot, gently dredge one of the crab cakes in the flour. Gently tap off the excess flour and add the crab cake to the pan; repeat with the remaining crab cakes, then turn the heat to medium-high.

3. Cook, rotating the cakes in the pan as necessary to brown the first side, 5 to 8 minutes. Turn and brown the other side, which will take slightly less time. Serve hot with lemon wedges.

Wine: A lesser Cabernet or Bordeaux, Pinot Noir, or lighter wine from southern France

Serving: Serve with Simple Green Salad (Vegetables, page 10) or any green salad with whatever sauce you are serving with the crab cakes (thinned a bit, if necessary, to use as salad dressing), or Tomato Salad with Basil (Vegetables, page 20).

Soups

Cold Tomato Soup with Rosemary

Good tomatoes are bursting with potential. The difference between consuming a tomato out of hand and slicing it, then sprinkling it with a pinch of salt and a few drops of olive oil, is the difference between a snack and a dish. And the great thing about tomatoes is that it takes so little to convert them from one to the other.

This soup is a great example, an almost instant starter that requires no cooking at all. It benefits from a period of chilling after being put together, but if you use ice cubes in place of chicken stock (or combine the two), you can even skip that.

Makes: 4 servings

Time: 15 minutes, plus time to chill

2 slices good stale white bread, crusts removed

3 pounds ripe tomatoes, peeled, seeded, and roughly chopped

1 teaspoon fresh rosemary leaves

1 small garlic clove, peeled

1 cup chicken stock or ice cubes

Salt and freshly ground black pepper

Juice of 1 lemon, or more to taste

1. Soak the bread in cold water briefly; squeeze dry and combine in a blender with the tomatoes, rosemary, and garlic (you may have to do this in two batches). Add the ice cubes if using them. Turn on the machine and drizzle in the stock. Turn off the machine and pour the mixture into a bowl.

2. Season with salt and pepper to taste, then add lemon juice. Chill and serve.

Wine: Beaujolais, lightly chilled, or another light red

Serving: The perfect starter for a summer meal of almost anything; try, for example, Grilled Steaks with Roquefort Sauce, (Meat, Fish & Poultry, page 62).

Jean-Georges's Tomato-Melon Gazpacho

I like gazpacho, but the ultimate minimalist version—take a few tomatoes, a red pepper, some onion, oil, and vinegar, and whiz it in a blender—doesn't cut it for me. I find this pulverized salad coarse, its raw flavor strong and altogether too lingering.

The great chef, my friend and sometimes coauthor Jean-Georges Vongerichten, suggested that I abandon tradition entirely and combine tomatoes with another fruit of the season: cantaloupe. These, combined with basil and lemon—in place of vinegar—produce the mildest, most delicious, creamiest gazpacho I've ever tasted. With its bright orange color, it's also among the most beautiful.

Makes: 8 servings

Time: 1 hour, largely unattended

8 tomatoes, about 3 pounds

Two 3-pound cantaloupes or other melons

¼ cup olive oil

20 fresh basil leaves

Salt and freshly ground black pepper

Juice of 2 lemons

1. Core, peel, and seed the tomatoes; cut the flesh into 1-inch chunks. Seed the melons and remove the flesh from the rind; cut into chunks. Place 2 tablespoons of olive oil in each of two large skillets and turn the heat under both to high (you can do this sequentially if you prefer). Add the melon to one and the tomatoes to the other and cook, stirring, until they both become juicy, about 3 minutes.

2. Combine the melon and tomatoes in one skillet, then divide into two batches. In a blender, puree each batch with 10 basil leaves, 1½ cups water, and ½ cup ice cubes; season with salt and pepper. Chill, then add the lemon juice to taste and adjust the seasoning. Serve.

Wine: A full-bodied white, preferably a decent Burgundy

Serving: Definitely a starter, great before grilled meat and a salad

Pumpkin Soup

Usually, pumpkin means pie, a limited role for a large vegetable that is nearly ubiquitous from Labor Day through Christmas. But soup based on pumpkin—or other winter squash like acorn or butternut—is a minimalist's dream, a luxuriously creamy dish that requires little more than a stove and a blender.

Makes: 4 servings

Time: 40 minutes

---

2 pounds peeled pumpkin or other winter squash

4 to 5 cups chicken or other stock

Salt and freshly ground black pepper

1. Place the pumpkin or squash in a saucepan with stock to cover and a pinch of salt. Turn the heat to high and bring to a boil. Cover and adjust the heat so that the mixture simmers. Cook until the pumpkin or squash is very tender, about 30 minutes. If time allows, cool.

2. Place the mixture, in batches if necessary, in a blender and puree until smooth. (The recipe can be prepared a day or two in advance up to this point; cool, place in a covered container, and refrigerate.) Reheat, adjust the seasoning, and serve.

Wine: As long as it's white and dry, almost anything will do, from something light to a fine Burgundy.

Serving: This is a very homey starter to a fall meal and is perfect on Thanksgiving.

Pea and Ginger Soup

Fresh peas are inestimably better than frozen for munching, but by the time you cook them and mix them with ginger, they have lost much of their advantage. If you can't find them, or can't deal with them—the shelling does take a while—by all means use frozen.

Makes: 8 servings

Time: 30 minutes

4 cups fresh or frozen peas

¼ cup peeled and roughly chopped fresh ginger (or more to taste, up to ½ cup)

Salt and freshly ground black pepper

8 cups chicken or other stock

1. Combine all the ingredients in a saucepan and bring to a boil over medium-high heat. Reduce the heat to a simmer and cook until the peas and ginger are very tender, about 15 minutes. Cool for a few minutes.

2. Pour into a blender and carefully blend until pureed. Return to the pan, and, over medium-low heat, reheat gently, stirring occasionally. When the soup is hot, taste and adjust the seasoning and serve.

Wine: Almost always white, usually crisp and unpretentious; something inexpensive and clean

Serving: In summer, serve chilled with bread and salad for a light meal. In cold weather, serve warm as a hearty starter.

Asian-Style Cucumber Soup

For years I was stuck on blended or cooked cucumber soups, until I was served a clear, chunky, ice-cold soup laced with soy and the sour-sweet-salty-spicy combination characteristic of so much Southeast Asian cooking. After I duplicated that, it occurred to me to make a similar preparation with nam pla (fish sauce) and coconut milk, an equally spicy but wonderfully creamy concoction. I doubt I'll ever use either the blender or the stove to make cucumber soup again.

Makes: 4 servings

Time: 30 minutes

---

3 cups chicken stock, preferably chilled

2 medium cucumbers

3 tablespoons soy sauce

2 tablespoons rice or white wine vinegar

1 small chile, stemmed, seeded, and minced, or ¼ teaspoon cayenne, or to taste

2 teaspoons sugar

½ cup minced trimmed scallions, both white and green parts

1 cup chopped watercress or arugula (optional)

1 cup roughly chopped cilantro, mint, Thai basil, or a combination

1. If the chicken stock is not cold, throw it in the freezer while you prepare the cucumbers. Peel them, then cut them in half the long way; use a spoon to scoop out the seeds. Slice them as thinly as possible (a mandolin is ideal for this). Mix them in a bowl with the soy sauce, vinegar, chile, and sugar and let them sit, refrigerated, for about 20 minutes.

2. Add the stock, scallions, and watercress or arugula if you like, and stir. Taste and adjust the seasoning. Just before serving, garnish with the herbs.

Wine: A fruity Riesling or Gewürztraminer

Serving: Rice Salad with Peas and Soy (Pizza, Pasta & Grains, page 86) or any grain salad

Lemongrass-Ginger Soup with Mushrooms

You can find all of these ingredients at almost any supermarket, and if you don't have luck at yours, try an Asian market, where they are as common as carrots, celery, and onions. (And if you do go to an Asian market, pick up some rice or bean thread noodles, which require almost no cooking time and turn this dish into a meal.)

You don't need oyster mushrooms, by the way—fresh shiitakes or even white button mushrooms are just as good. All you really need to know is that lemongrass must be trimmed of its outer layers before being minced, and nam pla (fish sauce) keeps forever in your pantry (and tastes much better than it smells).

Makes: 4 servings

Time: 30 minutes

6 cups good-quality chicken stock

3 lemongrass stalks

4 nickel-sized slices peeled fresh ginger

3 to 4 small fresh hot chiles, minced (optional)

2 tablespoons nam pla (fish sauce), or to taste

6 to 8 ounces oyster mushrooms, roughly chopped

Salt (optional)

2 teaspoons minced lime leaves or lime zest

Juice of 1 lime

¼ cup minced fresh cilantro

1. Heat the stock over medium heat. Trim two of the lemongrass stalks of their toughest outer layers, then bruise them with the back of a knife; cut them into sections and add them to the stock with the ginger and about one-fourth of the chiles if you're using them. Simmer for about 15 minutes, longer if you have the time. (You can prepare the recipe in advance up to this point; cover and refrigerate for up to 2 days before proceeding.) Peel all the hard layers off the remaining stalk of lemongrass and mince its tender inner core.

2. When you're just about ready to eat the soup, remove the lemongrass and ginger. Add 1 tablespoon of the nam pla and the mushrooms. Taste the broth and add more chiles if you like, as well as some salt if necessary. In the bottom of each of 4 warmed bowls, sprinkle a little chile if using, lime leaves or zest, lime juice, cilantro, and minced lemongrass. Ladle the soup into the bowls and add a teaspoon of nam pla to each bowl. Serve piping hot.

Wine: Gewürztraminer or other fruity, off-dry white, or Champagne; or beer

Serving: This is a good starter for any stir-fry.

Nearly Instant Miso Soup with Tofu

This ultra-simplified miso soup is delicious. It can be used in place of stock in many recipes, although you have to take care, because it has much more character than most stocks.

"Real" miso soup is little more complicated, and begins with dashi, a basic Japanese stock made with kelp (kombu) and flakes of dried bonito (a relative of tuna). I simply whisk or blend a tablespoon of miso into a cup of water, and turn the soup into a meal by adding cubed tofu and some vegetables at the last moment. Instead of tofu, you might cook shrimp or boneless chicken into the soup for a couple of minutes.

Buy traditional, unpasteurized, even organic miso, which is common enough, inexpensive enough (it's tough to spend more than $8 on a pound of miso), and better than quick-made miso, which is comparable to quick-made Parmesan or quick-made wine. All miso has a long shelf life, keeping for at least several months in the refrigerator with little or no loss of quality.

Traditionally, thick, dark brown hatcho miso is used to make soup, but the lighter varieties, which are more often used to make dressings and sauces, are fine too.

Makes: 4 servings

Time: 15 minutes

⅓ cup dark or other miso

½ pound tofu, cut into ½-inch cubes

¼ cup minced carrot

¼ cup minced scallions, both white and green parts

1. Bring 6 cups of water to a boil in a medium saucepan. Turn the heat to low, then mix about ½ cup of the water with the miso in a bowl or blender; whisk or blend until smooth. (If you have an immersion blender, the fastest and easiest tool here, carry out this operation in a tall measuring cup.)

2. Pour the miso mixture back into the hot water and add the tofu and carrot; stir once or twice and let sit for a minute, just long enough to heat the tofu through. Add the scallions and serve.

Wine: Sake or not-too-dry Riesling

Serving: White or brown rice, grilled tofu or chicken breasts brushed with soy sauce

The Minimalist's Corn Chowder

Anyone who ever had a garden or raided a cornfield knows that when corn is young you can eat it cob and all and that the cob has as much flavor as the kernels. That flavor remains even when the cob has become inedibly tough, and you can take advantage of it by using it as the base of a corn chowder—a corn stock, if you will. Into that stock can go some starch for bulk, a variety of seasonings from colonial to contemporary, and, finally, the corn kernels. The entire process takes a half hour or a little bit longer, and the result is a thick, satisfying, late-summer chowder.

Makes: 4 servings

Time: 30 to 40 minutes

---

4 to 6 ears corn

1 tablespoon unsalted butter or neutral oil, like corn or grape seed

1 medium onion, chopped

2 medium potatoes, peeled and cut into ¼-inch pieces

Salt and freshly ground black pepper

2 tomatoes, seeded and chopped (optional)

1 cup milk

½ cup chopped fresh parsley (optional)

1. Shuck the corn and use a paring knife to strip the kernels into a bowl. (Catch any liquid that seeps out and add it to the soup.) Put the cobs in a pot with 1 quart water; bring to a boil, cover, and lower the heat to simmer while you continue.

2. Put the butter or oil in a saucepan and turn the heat to medium-high. When the butter melts or the oil is hot, add the onion and potatoes, along with a sprinkling of salt and pepper. Cook, stirring occasionally, until the onion softens, about 5 minutes; add the tomatoes if you're using them and cook, stirring, for another minute or two.

3. After the corn cobs have cooked for at least 10 minutes, strain the liquid into the onion-potato mixture; bring to a boil, then turn the heat down so the mixture simmers. When the potatoes are tender, after about 10 minutes, add the corn kernels and milk and heat through. Adjust the seasoning, garnish with the parsley if you like, and serve.

Wine: Pinot Grigio, Sauvignon Blanc, or any fresh, crisp white

Serving: Simple Green Salad (Vegetables, page 10) or any green salad, or Tomato Salad with Basil (Vegetables, page 20)

Cream of Spinach Soup

Always be careful when pureeing hot soup; if time allows, the safest route is to cool the soup thoroughly before pureeing it. If you're in a hurry, at least cool it to not much more than body temperature (resting the cooking pan in a larger one filled with ice water is the most efficient way to do this) before pureeing. To reduce the chance of spattering, pulse the blender on and off a couple of times before leaving it on, and hold the top down until you're sure it's not going anywhere.

Makes: 6 servings

Time: 30 minutes

---

2 pounds spinach, well washed and trimmed of thick stems
(or two 10-ounce packages frozen spinach, partially thawed)

2 large white onions, roughly chopped

6 cups chicken or other stock

A grating of nutmeg

Salt and freshly ground black pepper

2 cups heavy or light cream, half-and-half, or whole milk

1. Combine the spinach, onions, and stock in a large saucepan and turn the heat to medium-high. Bring to a boil, then lower the heat so the mixture barely bubbles and cook, stirring occasionally, until the spinach is very tender, about 10 minutes. Turn off the heat, add the nutmeg and a sprinkling of salt and pepper, and cool for a few minutes.

2. Working in batches, puree in a blender. Return to the pan, add the cream, and, over medium-low heat, reheat gently, stirring occasionally. When the soup is hot, taste and adjust the seasoning and serve.

Wine: Almost always white, usually crisp and unpretentious; something inexpensive and clean

Serving: In summer, serve chilled with bread and salad for a light meal. In cold weather, serve hot for a hearty starter.

Creamy Broccoli Soup

It isn't often that you can apply a simple formula to a broad range of dishes, but when it comes to creamy vegetable soups—whether hot or cold—there is one that actually works. The soups have three basic ingredients, and their proportions form a pyramid; three parts liquid, two parts vegetable, one part dairy.

The pyramid's foundation is chicken stock (you can substitute vegetable stock or water, but the result will be somewhat less substantial). The middle section is any vegetable, or combination of vegetables, that will puree nicely and produce good body and flavor. The peak is cream, or nearly any other dairy product—milk, yogurt, or sour cream.

Makes: 4 servings

Time: 30 minutes

2 cups broccoli florets and peeled stems
(about ½ average head), cut into chunks

3 cups chicken stock

1 garlic clove, peeled and cut in half

1 cup milk, cream, or yogurt

Salt and freshly ground black pepper

1. Combine the broccoli and the stock in a saucepan and simmer, covered, until the broccoli is tender, about 10 minutes. During the last minute or so of cooking, add the garlic (this cooks the garlic just enough to remove its raw taste). If you're serving the soup cold, chill now (or refrigerate for up to 2 days), or freeze for up to a month before proceeding).

2. Puree in a blender, in batches if necessary, until very smooth. Stir in the milk, cream, or yogurt and reheat gently (or chill again); do not boil. Season to taste and serve.

Wine: Almost always white, usually crisp and unpretentious; something inexpensive and clean

Serving: In summer, serve chilled with bread and salad for a light meal. In cold weather, these are hearty starters.

Creamy Mushroom Soup

The best-tasting dried mushrooms are dried porcini (also called cèpes), which have come down about 50 percent in price over the last few years (do not buy less than an ounce or so at a time—you can buy them by the pound, too—or you'll be paying way too much).

Or you can start with inexpensive dried shiitakes, readily available in Asian markets (where they're also called black mushrooms), or any other dried fungus, or an assortment. An assortment of fresh mushrooms is best, but you can simply rely on ordinary button (white) mushrooms or shiitakes (whose stems, by the way, are too tough to eat).

Makes: 4 servings

Time: 30 minutes

---

2 ounces dried mushrooms, about 1 cup

2 tablespoons unsalted butter

6 to 8 ounces fresh mushrooms, trimmed and sliced

Salt and freshly ground black pepper

2 tablespoons chopped shallot

1 cup heavy cream

2 teaspoons fresh lemon juice, or to taste

Chopped fresh chervil or parsley for garnish (optional)

1. Put the dried mushrooms in a saucepan with 5 cups water; bring to a boil, cover, turn the heat to low, and simmer for about 10 minutes, or until tender.

2. Meanwhile, put the butter in a skillet and turn the heat to medium-high. When the butter melts, add the sliced fresh mushrooms and turn the heat to high. Cook, stirring occasionally and seasoning with salt and pepper, until they give up their liquid and begin to brown, about 5 minutes. When the dried mushrooms are tender, scoop them from the liquid with a slotted spoon and add them to the skillet along with the shallot. When all the fresh mushrooms are browned and the shallot is tender, about 3 minutes later, turn off the heat.

3. Strain the mushroom-cooking liquid through a strainer lined with a cheesecloth or towel; measure it and add water or stock to make 1 quart. Rinse the saucepan and return the liquid to it. Add the mushrooms and cream and heat through; taste and adjust the seasoning. Add the lemon juice, taste once more, garnish with herbs if you like, and serve.

Wine: Dry sherry would be ideal, or a big, bright Chardonnay from Burgundy or California.

Serving: A rich soup that, with 60-Minute Bread (Pizza, Pasta & Grains, page 72) or good store-bought bread and Simple Green Salad (Vegetables, page 10), could be a meal. Or follow it with a light main course of chicken or fish.

Mushroom Barley Soup

A good mushroom barley soup needs no meat, because you can make it with dried porcini, which can be reconstituted in hot water in less than ten minutes, giving you not only the best-tasting mushrooms you can find outside of the woods but an intensely flavored broth that rivals beef stock. A touch of soy sauce is untraditional but really enhances the flavor.

Makes: 4 servings

Time: 45 minutes

¾ ounce dried porcini, about ¾ cup

2 tablespoons extra virgin olive oil

¼ pound shiitake or button (white) mushrooms, stemmed and roughly chopped

2 medium carrots, sliced

¾ cup pearled barley

Salt and freshly ground black pepper

1 bay leaf

1 tablespoon soy sauce

1. Soak the porcini in 1 quart of very hot water. Put the olive oil in a medium saucepan and turn the heat to high. Add the shiitakes and carrots and cook, stirring occasionally, until they begin to brown. Add the barley and continue to cook, stirring frequently, until it begins to brown; sprinkle with a little salt and pepper. Remove the porcini from their soaking liquid (do not discard the liquid); sort through and discard any hard bits.

2. Add the porcini to the pot and cook, stirring, for about a minute. Add the bay leaf, the mushroom-soaking water, and 5 cups additional water (or stock if you prefer). Bring to a boil, then lower the heat and simmer until the barley is very tender, 20 to 30 minutes. If the soup is very thick, add a little more water. Add the soy sauce, then taste and add more salt if necessary and plenty of pepper. Serve hot.

Wine: Cabernet from Bordeaux or a relatively fruity choice from California

Serving: This is a great starter for a hearty midwinter meal. Follow with Fastest Roasted Chicken (Meat, Fish & Poultry, page 43) and Pilaf with Pine Nuts and Currants (Pizza, Pasta & Grains, page 84).

Pan-Roasted Asparagus Soup with Tarragon

You can save yourself some time by using thin asparagus; if you use thicker stalks, peel them first or the soup will be fibrous.

Makes: 8 servings

Time: 45 minutes

---

3 pounds thin asparagus

4 tablespoons unsalted butter or extra virgin olive oil

20 fresh tarragon leaves, or 1 teaspoon dried

8 cups chicken or other stock

Salt and freshly ground black pepper

1. Break off the bottom part of each asparagus stalk and discard. Coarsely chop the rest of the stalks, leaving about twenty-five of the flower ends whole. Put the butter in a large, deep skillet or broad saucepan and turn the heat to medium-high. A minute later, add the asparagus and tarragon, raise the heat to high, and cook, stirring only occasionally, until nicely browned, about 10 minutes. Remove the whole flower ends; set aside.

2. Add the stock and some salt and pepper; bring to a boil, then reduce the heat and simmer until the asparagus is very tender, about 10 minutes. Cool for a few minutes.

3. Use a blender to carefully puree, in batches. Return to the pan and, over medium-low heat, reheat gently, stirring occasionally. When the soup is hot, taste and adjust the seasoning. Put three or four of the cooked flower ends in each of 8 bowls; ladle in the soup and serve.

Wine: A light Pinot Noir (red Burgundy) or another fruity red, like Beaujolais; or a good Chardonnay (white Burgundy) or other sturdy white

Serving: Serve in the spring as an appetizer for Broiled Salmon with Beurre Noisette (Meat, Fish & Poultry, page 8).

Curried Sweet Potato Soup with Apricot

Make this soup even richer and sweeter by using half chicken stock and half canned coconut milk.

Makes: 8 servings

Time: About 1 hour

---

2 tablespoons unsalted butter

1 tablespoon curry powder, or to taste

2 large sweet potatoes, about 2 pounds, peeled and cut into chunks

2 cups dried apricots, about 1 pound

Salt

8 cups chicken or other stock

1. Put the butter in a flameproof casserole or Dutch oven and turn the heat to medium-high; when the butter melts, add the curry and cook, stirring, for about 30 seconds. Add the sweet potatoes and the apricots and cook, stirring occasionally, until well mixed, a minute or so.

2. Season with salt and add the stock. Turn the heat to high and bring to a boil. Cover and adjust the heat so that the mixture simmers. Cook until the potatoes are very tender, 20 to 30 minutes. If time allows, cool.

3. Place the mixture, in batches if necessary, in a blender and puree until smooth, adding a little water or stock if necessary if the mixture is too thick. (The recipe can be prepared a day or two in advance up to this point; cool, place in a covered container, and refrigerate.) Reheat, adjust the seasoning, and serve.

Wine: Beer or a chilled Pinot Noir or Beaujolais would be terrific.

Serving: Serve with Coconut Rice and Beans (Pizza, Pasta & Grains, page 80).

Vichyssoise with Garlic

In its traditional form, this cold potato-and-leek soup borders on boring: potatoes, leeks (or onions, or a combination), water or stock, salt and pepper, butter, and cream. What little complexity the soup has comes from lightly browning the vegetables in the butter, using lots of salt and pepper, good stock, and, of course, the cream. But if you add other vegetables, like garlic and carrots, things become more interesting. And you can nudge the soup over into gazpacho territory by adding a tomato to the mix, along with basil. Some protein, like shrimp, makes it even more of a whole-meal soup.

Makes: 4 servings

Time: 40 to 60 minutes, plus time to chill

4 cups water, stock, or a combination

1 pound potatoes, peeled and cut into slices or chunks

1 pound leeks or onions or a combination (leeks well-washed and onions peeled), cut into slices or chunks

1 whole head green garlic, plus its stem, chopped into pieces, or 3 garlic cloves, peeled

Salt and freshly ground black pepper

½ to 1 cup heavy cream or half-and-half

Chopped parsley, chervil, or chives

1. Combine the water or stock, potatoes, leeks, garlic, salt, and pepper in a saucepan, cover, and turn the heat to high. Bring to a boil, then lower the heat so the mixture simmers steadily but not violently. Cook until the potatoes are tender, 20 to 30 minutes. Cool or chill, then season to taste.

2. Puree in a blender, then chill fully. Stir in the cream, then taste and adjust the seasoning and serve, garnished with parsley.

Wine: Good Chardonnay, preferably Chablis

Serving: Serve with 60-Minute Bread (Pizza, Pasta & Grains, page 72) or good store-bought bread.

Stracciatella

Egg drop soup, a cliché in American-Chinese restaurants for at least fifty years, has a less-well-known Italian counterpart called stracciatella. Both are based on the simple fact that eggs scramble or curdle in boiling water or stock, and each demonstrates the ease with which a basic dish can be transformed in spirit, moving from one cuisine to the other almost as quickly as you can change your mind about which you prefer.

Makes: 4 servings

Time: 15 minutes

---

4 cups chicken stock

4 eggs

¼ cup freshly grated Parmigiano-Reggiano cheese, plus (optional) a little more for garnish

A tiny grating of fresh nutmeg

2 tablespoons minced fresh parsley

Salt and freshly ground black pepper

1. Bring 3 cups of the stock to a boil in a 6- to 8-cup saucepan over medium-high heat. Beat the remaining stock with the eggs, cheese, nutmeg, and parsley until well blended.

2. When the stock is boiling, adjust the heat so that it bubbles frequently but not furiously. Add the egg mixture in a steady stream, stirring all the while. Stir occasionally until the eggs gather in small curds, 2 or 3 minutes.

3. Add salt and pepper to taste, then serve. Garnish with a little more cheese if you like.

Wine: A hearty red like Barolo (or anything else made with the Nebbiolo grape) or Cabernet

Serving: Serve as a starter before pasta or simply cooked meat, chicken, or fish.

Garlic Soup with Shrimp

Use stock in place of water if you have it. This is a fine place for canned stock, because the garlic-scented oil will boost it to a higher level.

Remember to cook the garlic very gently to add complexity and color; by then browning the bread in the same oil, you increase its flavor immeasurably. Also consider doubling the amount of bread given in the recipe here; like me, you may find the allure of bread crisped in garlic-scented oil irresistible.

Makes: 4 servings

Time: 30 minutes

¼ cup extra virgin olive oil

8 to 16 medium to large garlic cloves, peeled

Salt and freshly ground black pepper

4 thick slices French or Italian bread

6 cups shrimp stock, chicken stock, water, or a combination

1 to 1½ pounds shrimp, peeled

Minced fresh parsley for garnish (optional)

1. Combine the olive oil and garlic in a deep skillet or broad saucepan, turn the heat to medium, and sprinkle lightly with salt and pepper. Cook, turning the garlic cloves occasionally, until they are tender and lightly browned all over, about 10 minutes; lower the heat if they seem to be browning too quickly. Remove the garlic with a slotted spoon.

2. Turn the heat to low and add the bread (in batches if necessary); cook on each side until nicely browned, a total of about 4 minutes. Remove the bread, add the stock, and raise the heat to medium-high.

3. When the stock is nearly boiling, add the shrimp and salt and pepper to taste. Cook until the shrimp are pink, about 4 minutes. Put a piece of bread and a portion of garlic in each of 4 bowls, then ladle in a portion of soup and shrimp. Sprinkle with the parsley if desired and serve.

Wine: Chianti, Zinfandel, or a rough red from the south of France

Serving: Serve with a salad for a nice light dinner.

Prosciutto Soup

Water-based soups are great, but soups with character are best when made with meat stocks. Of course you don't always have stock, and there are shortcuts that produce in-between soups. One of the easiest and most effective ways of making a potent soup quickly and without stock is to start with a small piece of prosciutto or other dry-cured ham, like Smithfield. The long aging process this meat undergoes— almost always a year or more— ensures an intense flavor that is quickly transferred to anything in which it is cooked, including water.

Makes: 4 servings

Time: 20 minutes

---

3 tablespoons extra virgin olive oil

¼ pound prosciutto, in 1 chunk or slice

4 garlic cloves

1 medium onion

½ pound greens, such as spinach or kale

¾ cup small pasta, such as orzo or small shells

Salt and freshly ground black pepper

1. Set 6 cups water to boil. Put 2 tablespoons of the olive oil in the bottom of a medium saucepan and turn the heat to medium. Chop the prosciutto (remove the fat if you must, but remember that it has flavor) into ¼-inch or smaller cubes, and add to the oil. Brown, stirring occasionally, for about 5 minutes, while you prepare the garlic, onion, and greens.

2. Chop the garlic roughly or leave it whole. Chop the onion. Wash the greens and chop into bite-sized pieces.

3. When the prosciutto has browned, add the garlic and cook, stirring occasionally, until it begins to color, about 2 minutes. Add the onion and cook, stirring occasionally, until it becomes translucent, 2 or 3 minutes. Add the greens and stir, then add the 6 cups boiling water. (You can prepare the dish in advance up to this point. Cover and refrigerate for up to 2 days, then reheat before proceeding.) Stir in the pasta and a good sprinkling of salt and pepper; adjust the heat so the mixture simmers.

4. When the pasta is done, taste and add more salt and pepper if necessary. Drizzle with the remaining 1 tablespoon olive oil and serve.

Wine: Rough and red, like Chianti

Serving: As you can see from the above, it's easy enough to make this into something approaching a whole-meal soup, in which case all you need is some bread.

Black-Eyed Pea Soup with Ham and Watercress

The soup draws its main flavors from olive oil, cured meat, and watercress. It gains substance and supporting flavors from the peas and a little onion. The combination is delicious, warming, and celebratory in a rustic way.

Makes: 4 servings

Time: 40 to 60 minutes

2 tablespoons extra virgin olive oil

2 ounces ham or prosciutto, chopped

1 medium onion, chopped

2 cups cooked, canned, or frozen black-eyed peas

2 cups washed, trimmed and chopped watercress

Salt and freshly ground black pepper

1. Pour 1 tablespoon of the oil into a deep skillet or casserole and turn the heat to medium-high. Add the meat and cook, stirring, for a minute; then add the onion and cook, stirring occasionally, until it softens and begins to brown, about 10 minutes.

2. Add the peas and 4 cups water and bring to a boil; turn the heat to medium-low and simmer, uncovered, until the peas are completely tender—10 minutes for cooked or canned peas, about 30 minutes for frozen.

3. Stir in the watercress, season with salt and pepper, and cook, stirring occasionally, for just a couple of minutes, or until it wilts. Add more water, if necessary. Taste and adjust the seasoning, stir in the remaining 1 tablespoon oil, and serve.

Wine: Chianti or another light red

Serving: Serve with Corn Bread (Pizza, Pasta & Grains, page 73), 60-Minute Bread (Pizza, Pasta & Grains, page 72), or good store-bought bread.

Chickpea Soup with Sausage

The cooking liquid of chickpeas, unlike that of most other beans, tastes so good that it makes the basis of a decent soup. Season the beans and their stock as they cook—with garlic, herbs, and some aromatic vegetables, for example—and you have the start of a great soup. Puree some of the cooked chickpeas, then stir them back into the soup, and it becomes deceptively, even sublimely, creamy.

Makes: 4 servings

Time: 2 hours

1½ cups dried chickpeas

5 garlic cloves, sliced, plus 1 teaspoon minced garlic

3 fresh rosemary or thyme sprigs

1 medium to large carrot, cut into small dice

1 celery stalk, trimmed and cut into small dice

1 medium onion, cut into small dice

Salt and freshly ground black pepper

½ pound sausage, grilled or broiled and thinly sliced (optional)

1 tablespoon extra virgin olive oil, or to taste

1. If you have the time, soak the chickpeas for several hours or overnight in water to cover (if not, don't worry). Combine the chickpeas, sliced garlic, and herbs in a large saucepan with fresh water to cover by at least 2 inches. Bring to a boil, turn down the heat, and simmer, partially covered, for at least 1 hour, or until fairly tender. Add water if it is boiling off and skim any foam that rises to the top of the pot.

2. Scoop out the herbs and add the carrot, celery, onion, salt, and pepper to the pot. Continue to cook until the chickpeas and vegetables are soft, at least another 20 minutes. Remove about half the chickpeas and vegetables and carefully puree in a blender with enough of the water to allow the machine to do its work. Return the puree to the soup and stir; reheat with the minced garlic, adding water if the mixture is too thick.

3. Stir in the sausage if you are using it and cook for a few minutes longer. Taste and adjust the seasoning, then serve, drizzled with the olive oil.

Wine: Chianti, a red from the south of France, or any other light but assertive red

Serving: Serve with 60-Minute Bread (Pizza, Pasta & Grains, page 72) or good store-bought bread and Roasted Red Peppers (Vegetables, page 58).

Rich Chicken Noodle Soup with Ginger

Buy rice "vermicelli," the thinnest rice noodles sold. Substitute angel hair pasta (you'll have to boil it separately) if you like.

Makes: 4 servings

Time: 30 minutes

Scant ½ pound fine rice noodles

6 cups chicken stock

1 small dried chile

1 tablespoon finely minced peeled fresh ginger

1 bunch of scallions

½ pound skinless, boneless chicken breast, cut into ½-inch cubes

¼ pound fresh shiitake mushrooms, stems removed, caps sliced

2 tablespoons nam pla (fish sauce) or soy sauce, or to taste

Salt if necessary

¼ cup roughly chopped fresh cilantro

1. Soak the rice noodles in very hot water to cover. Meanwhile, put the stock in a saucepan with the chile and ginger over medium heat. Trim the scallions; chop the white part and add it to the simmering stock. Chop the green part and set aside.

2. After about 8 minutes of simmering, remove the chile. Drain the noodles and add them, along with the chicken breast and mushrooms. Stir and adjust the heat so the mixture continues to simmer. When the chicken is cooked through, about 10 minutes, add the nam pla; taste and adjust the seasoning—add more nam pla or soy sauce or some salt if necessary, along with the cilantro and reserved scallions, then serve.

Wine: Dry (fino) sherry or beer

Serving: This is a satisfying meal on its own.

Roasted Chestnut Soup

Chestnuts have a subtle but distinctive flavor; another, less-well-known attribute is their ability to lend a rich, creamy texture to anything in which they're pureed—making cream completely superfluous. This soup is a perfect example, and if you can find frozen, peeled chestnuts, it's the work of a moment. But even if you cannot, the chestnut-peeling process takes about 20 minutes start to finish, and much of that time is unattended; you can use it to chop and cook the vegetables.

Makes: 4 servings

Time: 45 to 60 minutes

---

10 large chestnuts, peeled or unpeeled

2 tablespoons extra virgin olive oil or butter

2 cups chopped celery

½ cup chopped onion

Salt and freshly ground black pepper

4 cups good chicken stock

Chopped celery leaves or parsley

1. If you have peeled chestnuts, proceed to step 2. If your chestnuts still have their skins, preheat the oven to 350° F. Use a sharp (preferably curved) paring knife to make an "X" on their flat sides. Bake them in an open pan for 10 to 15 minutes, or until their peels begin to open away from the meat. They will then be easy to peel; remove both outer and inner skins while they are warm. (The peeled chestnuts will cook faster if you chop them roughly, but it isn't necessary).

2. Meanwhile (if you have peeled chestnuts, start here), pour the olive oil into a deep skillet or casserole, turn the heat to medium, and heat for a couple of minutes. Add the celery, onion, and a good sprinkling of salt and pepper. Cook, stirring occasionally, until the onion is translucent, about 10 minutes. Add the stock and the chestnuts, bring to a boil, and partially cover. Adjust the heat so that the mixture simmers and cook until the chestnuts are mushy, about 30 minutes.

3. Carefully puree the soup in a blender (if you are not in a hurry, cool it slightly first for extra caution). Measure and add sufficient water to total 6 cups of liquid. Reheat, adjust the seasoning if necessary, garnish, and serve.

Wine: Bordeaux or another big red

Serving: 60-Minute Bread (Pizza, Pasta & Grains, page 72) or good store-bought bread; Roasted Red Peppers (Vegetables, page 58); Glazed Carrots (Vegetables, page 61)

Cauliflower Curry with Chicken

There's a more-or-less standard Indian dish of cauliflower and potatoes that to me, despite its lovable flavors, is simply too starchy. Substitute boneless chicken for the potatoes, however, and the preparation turns into a one-dish meal, increasing both its appeal and its usefulness. The chewiness of the chicken—as opposed to the mealiness of the potatoes—gives the dish an added dimension.

Makes: 4 servings

Time: 40 minutes

2 tablespoons peanut, grape seed, or other oil

½ cup minced onion

1 head cauliflower (about 2 pounds)

1 tablespoon cumin seeds, optional

2 teaspoons curry powder, or to taste

5 or 6 canned plum tomatoes, with their juice

Salt and freshly ground black pepper

1 pound boneless, skinless chicken, cut into ½-inch cubes

Juice of 1 lemon

Minced fresh parsley or cilantro, optional

1. Pour the oil into a 12-inch skillet and turn the heat to high; add the onion and cook, stirring occasionally, until it begins to brown, about 5 minutes. While the onion is cooking, trim the cauliflower and cut the florets into ½-inch-thick pieces.

2. When the onion has browned a little, add the cumin seeds and curry and cook for about 30 seconds. Add the cauliflower and stir, still over high heat, for another minute. Cut up the tomatoes and add them, along with their juice, ¼ cup water, and a generous sprinkling of salt and pepper. Cover and turn the heat to medium-low.

3. Cook for 10 minutes, stirring once or twice, or until the cauliflower is beginning to become tender. Add the chicken, stir, cover, and cook for another 6 to 8 minutes until the chicken is cooked through. (If the sauce threatens to dry out at any point, add a little more water.) Stir in the lemon juice, taste and adjust the seasoning, garnish with parsley, if you like, and serve.

Wine: Beer or Zinfandel

Serving: Any flatbread or Pilaf with Pine Nuts and Currants (Pizza, Pasta & Grains, page 84)

Curried Tofu with Soy Sauce

Over the years, almost despite myself, I have become increasingly fond of tofu, not for its flavor—which is so subtle as to be almost nonexistent, especially in a full-flavored dish like this one—but for its silken, creamy texture. Given that tofu does not add much body to a dish, you need a substantial sauce, like one with canned coconut milk as its base. Like heavy cream, coconut milk will thicken a sauce, making it luxurious in almost no time.

Makes: 4 servings

Time: 20 to 30 minutes

2 tablespoons peanut, grape seed, or other oil

1 large onion, minced

1 tablespoon curry powder, or to taste

1 cup roughly chopped walnuts or unsalted cashews

One 12- to 14-ounce can (1½ to 2 cups) unsweetened coconut milk or 2 cups homemade coconut milk

1 block tofu (about 1 pound), cut into ¾-inch cubes

2 tablespoons soy sauce, or to taste

Salt

Cayenne pepper

1. Put the oil in a 10- or 12-inch nonstick skillet, turn the heat to medium-high, and heat for 1 minute. Add the onion and cook, stirring occasionally, until the edges of onion pieces are well-browned, about 10 minutes (for best flavor, the onions must brown but not burn). Add the curry powder and cook, stirring, for 30 seconds or so; add the nuts and cook, stirring occasionally, for about 1 minute.

2. Add the coconut milk. Stir, bring to a boil, and reduce the heat to medium. Add the tofu, stir, and let the tofu heat through for about 3 minutes. Stir in the soy, then taste and adjust the seasoning with soy, salt, and/or cayenne as necessary. Serve.

Wine: A not-too-dry Riesling

Serving: Brown or white rice, and, if you like, steamed vegetables

Clam Chowder

Although clam chowder takes many guises, the best is a simple affair that has as its flavorful essence the juices of the clams themselves. Of course, what is actually "essential" in clam chowder is debatable: Manhattanites, in theory at least, prefer theirs with tomatoes. New Englanders, we assume, like it with cream. There is also Rhode Island clam chowder, which in spirit at least is closest to the minimalist ideal: It contains clams, onion, celery, water, salt, and pepper.

Makes: 4 servings

Time: 30 minutes

At least 3 dozen littleneck clams (3 pounds or more) or an equivalent amount of other clams

1 medium onion, peeled and minced

2 large potatoes (about 1 pound), peeled and cut into ½-inch dice

Salt and freshly ground black pepper

1. Wash the clams well, scrubbing if necessary to remove external grit. Place them in a pot with ½ cup water and turn the heat to high. Steam, shaking the pot occasionally, until most of the clams are open, 7 to 10 minutes. Use a slotted spoon to remove the clams to a broad bowl; reserve the cooking liquid.

2. When the clams are cool enough to handle, shuck them over the bowl, catching every drop of their liquid; discard the shells. If any clams remain closed, use a thin-bladed knife to pry them open (the clams should be easy to open).

3. Chop the clams. Strain all the liquid through a sieve lined with a paper towel or a couple of layers of cheesecloth. Measure the liquid and add enough water to make 3½ cups. (You may prepare the dish in advance up to this point; refrigerate, covered, for up to a day before reheating.)

4. Combine the liquid with the onion and potatoes in a saucepan; cover and bring to a boil. Reduce to a simmer, still covered, and cook until the potatoes are tender, about 10 minutes. Stir in the clams, season to taste with salt and pepper, and serve.

Wine: Chardonnay, not necessarily an expensive one, is best.

Serving: A great starter for any seafood meal, especially Broiled Salmon with Beurre Noisette (Meat, Fish & Poultry, page 8).

Turkey Stock

Most turkey meat finds its way into sandwiches, but many cooks make a turkey soup as well, tossing the bones with some of the leftover meat into a pot with water to cover and simmering until the meat falls off the bones—a technique that produces quite decent results.

However, there's a nearly-as-simple method that allows you to produce dark, rich turkey stock in the turkey roasting pan. This broth has a broader range of uses than the throw-everything-in-the-pot variety; in fact, the result is very close to jus roti, the dark stock of classic French cooking.

Makes: About 2 quarts

Time: About 2½ hours, largely unattended

Bones, leftover meat, and carcass from a 15-pound turkey

2 carrots, peeled and cut into chunks

1 large onion, peeled and quartered

1 celery stalk, roughly chopped

1. Preheat the oven to 450° F. Place the bones, meat, and chopped carcass in a large roasting pan and put in the oven. Roast, stirring occasionally, for about 1 hour, or until nicely browned. Don't worry if the meat sticks to the bottom of the pan.

2. Add the chopped vegetables and roast for about 30 minutes more, stirring once or twice.

3. Move the roasting pan to the stovetop and place it over one or two burners, whichever is more convenient. Turn the heat to high and add water to barely cover the bones, about 8 to 10 cups; don't worry if some of the bones poke up out of the water. When the water boils, turn the heat down so that the liquid simmers.

4. Cook, stirring occasionally and scraping the bottom of the pan to loosen any bits of meat, for about 30 minutes. Cool, then strain. Refrigerate and skim off excess fat, then store for up to 3 days in the refrigerator (longer if you bring the stock to a boil every second day) or several months in the freezer.

Wine: The broth itself can be served with a good white or red Burgundy, or even a slightly sweet wine. If you add to it, choose a wine suited to the character of the additions.

Serving: This broth can go in many directions, but serves as a nice base to Mushroom Barley Soup (page 60) or minestrone.

Index

About the Author

Mark Bittman created and wrote the weekly *New York Times* column "The Minimalist," which ran for thirteen years. He currently covers food policy and all topics related to eating in a weekly op-ed column for the *New York Times*, and is the lead writer for the *Eat* column in the Sunday *New York Times Magazine*.

Bittman has written more than a dozen cookbooks, including *The Minimalist Cooks at Home*, *The Minimalist Cooks Dinner*, *The Minimalist Entertains*, as well as the popular family of kitchen standards *How to Cook Everything*, *How to Cook Everything Vegetarian*, and *How to Cook Everything The Basics*. Bittman explores global cuisines in *The Best Recipes in the World*, an inspired collection of recipes culled from his international travels. With Jean-Georges Vongerichten, he coauthored *Jean-Georges* (winner of a James Beard Award) and *Simple to Spectacular*. And his bestselling *Food Matters* and *Food Matters Cookbook* offer simple ways to improve your diet and the health of the planet.

As a longtime feature on commercial and public television, Bittman has hosted three award-winning cooking series on PBS, is often invited to share his viewpoints on news and magazine programs, and appears regularly on the *Today* show. He also records a weekly web video for the magazine, revisiting recipes from the beloved Minimalist column. For more information, visit www.markbittman.com.

Notes

Mark Bittman
The Mini Minimalist

**The Mini Minimalist
Meat, Fish & Poultry**

Meat, Fish & Poultry

Clarkson Potter/Publishers
New York

Based on the following books
by Mark Bittman: *The Minimalist
Cooks at Home,* copyright
© 2000 by Mark Bittman;
The Minimalist Cooks Dinner,
copyright © 2001 by Mark
Bittman; and *The Minimalist
Entertains,* copyright © 2003
by Mark Bittman.

Printed in China

Written by Mark Bittman

Design by Jan Derevjanik

Contents

Fish

Broiled Salmon with Beurre Noisette

Nothing like a little butter to jazz up a simple dish, and the complexity of browned butter—beurre noisette—really makes it happen.

Makes: 8 servings

Time: 20 minutes

Eight 6-ounce salmon steaks (or use fillets of red snapper or other sturdy, white-fleshed fish)

Salt and freshly ground black pepper

8 tablespoons (1 stick) unsalted butter

2 tablespoons fresh lemon juice

Minced fresh parsley, chervil, dill, chives, or scallions (optional)

1. Preheat the broiler, adjusting the rack so that it is 4 to 6 inches from the heat source. Sprinkle the salmon with salt and pepper. Broil until the first side is nicely browned, about 5 minutes; turn and cook just 2 or 3 minutes on the other side, or until the fish is done to your liking.

2. While the fish is cooking, put the butter in a small saucepan and turn the heat to medium. Cook, swirling the pan occasionally, until the butter stops foaming and begins to brown. Remove from the heat immediately and season lightly with salt and pepper; keep warm if necessary.

3. To serve, stir the lemon juice into the butter and drizzle a little of it over each piece of fish. Garnish with an herb, if you like.

Wine: A light Pinot Noir (red Burgundy) or another fruity red, like Beaujolais; or a good Chardonnay (white Burgundy) or other sturdy white

Serving: Pan-Roasted Asparagus Soup with Tarragon (Small Plates & Soups, page 62), Pan-Crisped Potatoes (Vegetables, page 68)

Salmon and Tomatoes Cooked in Foil

Cooking in packages requires a small leap of faith to decide that the food is done, because once you open the packages you want to serve them. This method works well.

Makes: 8 servings (4 packages)

Time: 40 minutes

½ cup extra virgin olive oil

3 to 4 pounds salmon fillet, cut crosswise into 8 pieces

12 cherry tomatoes, sliced in half

Salt and freshly ground black pepper

32 fresh basil leaves

1. Preheat the oven to 450°F. Put a baking pan large enough to hold the four foil packages in the oven while it preheats. Take eight sheets of aluminum foil, each about 18 inches long, and place one piece on top of another to make four double sheets. Smear the bottom of each with 1 tablespoon olive oil, then cover with 2 pieces of salmon, 6 tomato halves, some salt and pepper, 8 basil leaves, and another tablespoon of oil. Fold the foil onto itself and crimp the edges as tightly as possible. Repeat the process. (You can refrigerate the packages until you're ready to cook, but for no more than 6 hours.)

2. Put the packages in the baking dish and bake for about 15 minutes (or about 8 minutes from the time the packages start sizzling). Let sit for a couple of minutes before carefully slitting open each package and serving.

Wine: A big Chardonnay, like a well-oaked specimen from northern California, or a good white Burgundy

Serving: Bread Pudding with Shiitake Mushrooms (Pizza, Pasta & Grains, page 81), Big Chopped Salad with Vinaigrette (Vegetables, page 14)

Roast Salmon Steaks with Pinot Noir Syrup

I first had this mysterious, dark, extraordinarily delicious sauce at a Seattle restaurant called Brasa. It's a kind of gastrique, a relatively simple sauce that is based on caramelized sugar. Like many other foods—from coffee to bread to steak—sugar becomes somewhat bitter when browned, losing most if not all of its sweetness. In fact, it becomes markedly more complex, not only in flavor but also in molecular structure. This considerable change is not routine in most kitchens, but it's pretty easy to produce (and if you fail, you've only lost half a cup of sugar; try again, more slowly, and you'll get it).

Makes: 4 servings

Time: 40 to 50 minutes

½ cup sugar

2 cups Pinot Noir

1 sprig rosemary, plus 1 teaspoon chopped rosemary

4 salmon steaks, each about ½ pound

Salt and freshly ground black pepper

1 tablespoon balsamic vinegar

1 tablespoon unsalted butter

1. Preheat the oven to 450°F. Put the sugar in a heavy-bottomed saucepan, preferably nonstick and with rounded sides, and turn the heat to medium. Cook, without stirring (just shake the pan occasionally to redistribute the sugar) until the sugar liquefies and begins to turn

brown, about 10 minutes. Turn off the heat, stand back, and carefully add the wine. Turn the heat to high and cook, stirring, until the caramel dissolves again. Then add the rosemary sprig and reduce over high heat, stirring occasionally, until the mixture is syrupy and reduced to just over ½ cup, 10 to 15 minutes.

2. Heat an ovenproof nonstick skillet over high heat until it begins to smoke. Season the salmon on both sides with salt and pepper, then put it in the pan; immediately put the pan in the oven. Roast for 3 minutes, then turn the salmon and roast for another 3 minutes. Check to see that the salmon is medium-rare or thereabouts (it should still be orange in the center); cook for another 1 to 2 minutes if you like. Remove from the oven and keep it warm.

3. When the sauce is reduced, stir in the balsamic vinegar and butter and turn the heat to medium-low. Cook until the butter melts. Add salt and pepper and remove the rosemary sprig. Taste and adjust the seasoning, then serve over the fish. Garnish with the chopped rosemary.

Wine: Pinot Noir

Serving: 60-Minute Bread (Pizza, Pasta & Grains, page 72) or good store-bought bread, Steamed Broccoli with Beurre Noisette (Vegetables, page 32), Mashed Potatoes (Vegetables, page 74) or Pan-Crisped Potatoes (Vegetables, page 68)

Tuna au Poivre

Tuna au Poivre is yet another recipe that plays on tuna's similarity to beefsteak. How finely to grind the pepper is a matter of taste. Mine dictates "coarsely ground" as opposed to "cracked." That is, ground to the point where there are no large pieces left, but not to the point of powder. The coarser the grind, the more powerful the result will taste.

Makes: 8 servings

Time: 30 minutes

¼ cup coarsely ground black pepper

2 tablespoons extra virgin olive oil

Four 8- to 10-ounce tuna steaks, each at least 1 inch thick

Salt

4 tablespoons (½ stick) unsalted butter or additional olive oil

½ cup minced shallots

1½ cups dry red wine

1. Preheat the oven to 500°F; put the pepper on a flat plate. Place a large skillet, preferably nonstick, over medium-high heat; pour in the olive oil. Dredge both sides of each piece of tuna lightly in the pepper; it will adhere nicely, forming a thin coat. (Use a bit more pepper if necessary to coat.) As they're dredged, add the steaks to the pan (if you must use two pans, double the amount of oil); when they are all in, turn the heat to high. Cook for about 2 minutes, then turn; add salt and cook another minute. Turn the heat to low, transfer the steaks to a roasting pan, and place in the oven for at least 6 minutes.

2. Meanwhile, add half the butter to the pan (if you used two pans to brown the tuna, just use one to make the sauce), followed by the shallots. Lower the heat to medium and cook, stirring, until the shallots soften, about 2 minutes. Raise the heat to medium-high and add the wine; let it bubble away for a minute or so and add the remaining butter. Cook, stirring occasionally, until the butter melts and the sauce is thickened.

3. By this time the tuna will be medium-rare (cut into one to make certain). Cut the steaks in half, put each serving on a plate, and spoon a little sauce over it.

Wine: A powerful Cabernet or Bordeaux

Serving: Simple Green Salad (Vegetables, page 10), 60-Minute Bread (Pizza, Pasta & Grains, page 72)

Sautéed Red Snapper with Rhubarb Sauce

The addition of saffron not only adds a mysterious flavor but also gives the rhubarb a golden glow. Saffron is expensive, but not outrageous if bought in quantity; an ounce will last you years.

Makes: 8 servings

Time: 40 minutes

---

2 pounds rhubarb, rinsed and trimmed, strings removed

⅔ cup sugar, or more to taste

Large pinch of saffron (optional)

Salt and freshly ground black pepper

¼ cup extra virgin olive oil

4 tablespoons (½ stick) unsalted butter or additional olive oil

Eight 6-ounce red snapper fillets

Chopped fresh mint or parsley (optional)

1. Combine the rhubarb, sugar, and saffron, if you are using it, in a medium saucepan, cover, and turn the heat to low. Cook, stirring only occasionally, for about 20 minutes, or until the rhubarb becomes saucy. Add salt and pepper to taste and a little more sugar if necessary; if the mixture is very soupy continue to cook a little longer to thicken it.

2. When you judge the rhubarb to be nearly done, put a large skillet, preferably nonstick, over medium-high heat. (You can either use two skillets or cook in batches; undercook the first batch slightly and keep it warm in a 200°F oven while you cook the second batch.) A minute later, add the oil and butter (you may need a bit more of each if using two pans); when the butter foam subsides, add the fillets, skin side down. Cook for 4 to 5 minutes, or until the fish is nearly done; turn carefully and lightly brown the flesh side. Transfer to a plate lined with paper towels to absorb excess oil.

3. Serve the fish napped with a bit of the sauce and garnished, if you like, with the herb.

Wine: A crisp white would be best, such as a Chablis or comparable California Chardonnay, or even something lighter, like Pinot Grigio.

Serving: Raw Beet Salad (Vegetables, page 27), New Potatoes with Butter and Mint (Vegetables, page 72)

Roast Striped Bass with Tomatoes and Olives

Striped bass, one of our most firm-fleshed and delicious fish, is plentiful in the fall. Unlike many white-fleshed fish, it must be cooked through to become tender.

Makes: 8 servings

Time: 20 minutes

---

12 plum tomatoes, cut in half

¼ cup extra virgin olive oil

About 50 good, large black olives, such as kalamata (approximately 3 cups)

3 to 4 pounds striped bass fillet, skin on or off

Salt and freshly ground black pepper

Fresh thyme leaves (optional)

1. Preheat the oven to 500°F. Combine the tomatoes and half the olive oil in a small saucepan with 1 tablespoon water and the olives and cook over medium heat, stirring occasionally, until the mixture is saucy; keep warm.

2. Rub the fish all over with the remaining olive oil, then sprinkle with the salt and pepper. Place on a baking sheet or roasting pan, preferably nonstick, and put in the oven.

3. Roast the fish until a thin-bladed knife penetrates it with little resistance, about 10 minutes. When it is done, spoon the sauce over it, cut into 8 pieces, garnish with thyme, if desired, and serve.

Wine: You can go with a fruity red here, if you like—Pinot Noir, Zinfandel, or something similar—but a crisp, not-too-rich Chardonnay, especially from Chablis, is probably best.

Serving: Golden Pilaf with Saffron (Pizza, Pasta & Grains, page 82)

Broiled Bluefish or Mackerel with Green Tea Salt

Whether you have a "dedicated" spice grinder or a coffee grinder that you use occasionally for spices, it should be cleaned thoroughly before processing tea in it. There are two ways to do this (in either case, please remember to unplug the appliance before beginning). You can wipe it out well, first with a barely damp paper towel and then with a dry one. Or, grind a couple of tablespoons of rice to a powder, dispose of that, and then wipe with a paper towel.

Makes: 8 servings

Time: 15 minutes

About 3 pounds bluefish or mackerel fillets

2 tablespoons toasted sesame oil

2 tablespoons powdered green tea

1 tablespoon coarse salt

2 limes, quartered

1. Preheat the broiler; you want the heating element as close as possible to the surface of the fish, as little as 2 inches. Arrange the fish in a broiling pan, skin side down, and brush the surface lightly with sesame oil. Mix together the tea and salt.

2. Broil the fish, checking once or twice to make sure it is browning but not burning; lower the rack if necessary. When the fish is browned and a thin-bladed knife penetrates it with little resistance, it is done; total cooking time under a good broiler will be about 5 minutes.

3. Sprinkle the fish liberally with the tea-salt mixture and serve with lime wedges.

Wine: The flavors of Chardonnay and oak marry well with this dish; look for something from northern California.

Serving: Rich Chicken Noodle Soup with Ginger (Small Plates & Soups, page 78), Herbed Green Salad with Soy Vinaigrette (Vegetables, page 12)

Emma's Cod and Potatoes

Once, for a special occasion, I produced potatoes Anna for my daughter Emma, a dish in which potatoes are thin-sliced, drenched in butter, and roasted until golden—the ultimate in crisp potato dishes. This was a fatal error, because potatoes Anna are a pain to make, contain about a week's allotment of butter, and were forever in demand thereafter.

So I set about not only shortcutting the process, but also creating something approaching an entire meal. I cut back on the butter (when attacks of conscience strike I substitute olive oil) and enlisted the aid of the broiler in speeding the browning process. I figured that it would be just as easy to broil something on top of the potatoes during the last few minutes of cooking and, after a few tries, I found a thick fillet of fish to be ideal. The result is this simple weeknight dish that I now make routinely and that even impresses guests.

Makes: 4 servings

Time: 1 hour

4 or 5 medium potatoes, 2 pounds or more

6 tablespoons extra virgin olive oil or melted unsalted butter

Salt and freshly ground black pepper

1½ pounds cod or other white-fleshed fillets, about 1 inch thick (skinned), in 2 or more pieces

1. Preheat the oven to 400°F. Peel the potatoes and slice them about ⅛ inch thick (a mandolin comes in handy here). Toss the potatoes in an 8 x 11-inch or similar size baking pan with 4 tablespoons of the oil or butter. Season the potatoes liberally with salt and pepper, spread them evenly, and place the pan in the oven.

2. Cook for about 40 minutes, checking once or twice, until the potatoes are tender when pierced with a thin-bladed knife and have begun to brown on top. Turn on the broiler and adjust the rack so that it is 4 to 6 inches from the heat source.

3. Top the potatoes with the fish, drizzle with the remaining oil or butter, and sprinkle with some more salt and pepper. Broil until the fish is done, 6 to 10 minutes depending on its thickness (a thin-bladed knife will pass through it easily). If at any point the top of the potatoes begins to burn, move the pan a couple of inches farther away from the heat source.

Wine: A rich, full-bodied Chardonnay would cut it, or you could go with a light, fruity red, but a semiserious one, like Pinot Noir.

Serving: This is close to a meal in itself; add a salad or a vegetable (try Roasted Asparagus with Parmesan, Vegetables, page 45) and you're set.

Cod with Chickpeas and Sherry

An Andalusian dish with a sweet, aromatic sauce.

Makes: 8 servings

Time: 30 minutes with cooked or canned chickpeas

6 tablespoons olive oil

4 cod fillets, each about 1 inch thick, about 3 pounds total

Salt and freshly ground black pepper

6 cups cooked (or canned) chickpeas, with 1 cup reserved cooking liquid or water (if using canned chickpeas)

1½ cups Sherry, preferably Amontillado

¼ cup minced garlic

Chopped fresh parsley (optional)

1. Preheat the oven to 300°F. Put 3 tablespoons of the oil in a nonstick skillet large enough to hold the cod in one layer (cook in batches if necessary, but undercook the first batch by about a minute, as it will remain in the oven longer, and use more oil if necessary); turn the heat to medium-high. When the oil is hot, add the fish, skin side (it won't have skin, but will be shiny) up. Cook, undisturbed, for about 5 minutes, or until the cooked side is evenly browned. Turn the fish onto an ovenproof plate, browned side up, sprinkle with salt and pepper, and put it in the oven.

2. Immediately add the chickpeas (with about 1 cup of their liquid) to the skillet and cook, stirring, for about a minute. Add all but 2 tablespoons of the Sherry and raise the heat to high. Cook, shaking the pan now and then, until the liquid is all but evaporated and the chickpeas are beginning to brown, about 10 minutes. Stir in the garlic along with some salt and pepper and cook 1 minute, stirring occasionally; stir in the remaining olive oil and Sherry.

3. By this time the fish should be done. (A thin-bladed knife inserted into it should meet no resistance. If it is not done, hold the chickpeas over low heat until it is.) Serve the fish on top of the chickpeas, garnished with parsley, if you like.

Wine: Any fairly light red, from Beaujolais to a wine from southern France or a similar California blend

Serving: 60-Minute Bread (Pizza, Pasta & Grains, page 72) or good store-bought bread; Roasted Red Peppers (Vegetables, page 58) or Glazed Carrots (Vegetables, page 61)

Salt-Cured Cod with Arugula Sauce

Briefly salting fresh cod (or other delicate fish, like haddock, whiting, or sea trout) changes its texture slightly, and for the better: By removing just enough water to tighten the fillet's flesh, the salt enables you to poach the fish without worrying that it will fall apart.

Makes: 8 servings

Time: 1½ hours, largely unattended

Coarse salt as needed

3 to 4 pounds thick-cut cod fillet

2 bay leaves

4 to 5 cups milk, fish stock, or water

4 cups arugula or watercress (thin stems are okay)

8 scallions, trimmed

1. On a plate or tray large enough to hold the fish in one layer, evenly spread salt to a depth of about ⅛ inch. Lay the cod on it and cover it with another layer of salt. Let stand for about 45 minutes.

2. Rinse the fish well until no traces of salt remain. Put it in a pan just large enough to hold it in one layer, then add the bay leaves and enough milk to barely cover. Bring to a boil over high heat, then adjust the heat so the mixture simmers gently. The fish is done when a skewer or thin-bladed knife passes through it with little resistance, 5 to 10 minutes.

3. Meanwhile, combine the arugula and scallions in a blender with a small pinch of salt and some of the poaching liquid. Blend until creamy, adding a little more liquid if necessary. When the fish is done, drain it, remove and discard the bay leaves, and serve the cod with the sauce.

Wine: A straightforward white with a little body, like a Pinot Blanc

Serving: Simple Green Salad (Vegetables, page 10) and Persian Rice and Potatoes (Pizza, Pasta & Grains, page 76)

Roasted Bay Scallops with Brown Butter and Shallots

Real bay scallops—the kind that come mostly from Nantucket—are in season through the winter and are an amazing treat (they're also expensive). Though you can eat them raw, they're also good cooked, but simply . . . very simply. Substitute sea scallops, if you like, but if they're big, cut them into halves or quarters.

Makes: 8 servings

Time: 20 minutes

---

8 tablespoons (1 stick) unsalted butter

3 pounds bay or sea scallops

¼ cup minced shallots

Salt and freshly ground black pepper

Chopped fresh basil or snipped fresh chives

1. Preheat the oven to the maximum, at least 500°F. Put a roasting pan large enough to hold the scallops in one layer in the oven while it preheats. When the oven is hot, put the butter in the pan. Return to the oven, shaking the pan once or twice, until the butter melts and begins to turn brown.

2. Immediately add the scallops and roast in the oven, undisturbed, for about 3 minutes. Remove the pan, add the shallots, and stir. Return to the oven for about 2 minutes, or until the scallops are done (they should be tender and not at all rubbery; do not overcook). Season with salt and pepper, stir in the herb, and serve.

Wine: The best white you can lay your hands on, which almost always means a Burgundy, in this case something from the area of Montrachet or Meursault, if you can afford it

Serving: Garlic-Mushroom Flan (Pizza, Pasta & Grains, page 88), Endives Braised in Broth with Parmesan (Vegetables, page 34)

Chile-Fried Shrimp with Scallions and Oranges

How nicely the flavors of chiles and oranges complement one another in this dish, essentially an easy stir-fry. Note that you want fairly large pieces of orange, so stick with a vegetable peeler or paring knife; avoid as much of the bitter white pith as you can without getting obsessive about it.

Makes: 8 servings

Time: 20 minutes

2 oranges or large tangerines

2 tablespoons peanut or vegetable oil

4 small dried chiles, or to taste

3 pounds shrimp, peeled

Salt and freshly ground black pepper

16 scallions, trimmed and cut into 2-inch lengths

Sesame seeds

1. Use a vegetable peeler or paring knife to remove the zest from the oranges; roughly chop the zest. Cut the oranges and juice them; set the juice aside.

2. Put a large skillet over medium-high heat and add the oil. A minute later, add the chiles and orange zest. After a minute or two the chiles will start smoking; turn the heat to high and add the shrimp. Cook without stirring for about 2 minutes, then stir the shrimp and season with salt and pepper.

3. Add the scallions and cook, stirring occasionally, just until they begin to soften, about 2 minutes. Stir in the orange juice. Taste and adjust the seasoning if necessary, garnish with sesame seeds, and serve.

Wine: Beer or Champagne

Serving: 60-Minute Bread (Pizza, Pasta & Grains, page 72), Simple Green Salad (Vegetables, page 10), Tuna au Poivre (page 14)

Bouillabaisse

Bouillabaisse, the Mediterranean fish stew that is more difficult to spell than to prepare, is traditionally neither an idée fixe nor the centerpiece of a *grande bouffe,* but a spur-of-the-moment combination of the day's catch.

Makes: 8 servings

Time: 1 hour

1 tablespoon olive oil

2 medium onions, roughly chopped

2 navel or other oranges

2 teaspoons fennel seeds

Big pinch of saffron (optional)

1 dried chile or a pinch of cayenne, or to taste

2 cups chopped fresh or canned tomatoes

1 to 1½ pounds monkfish, catfish, or blackfish, cut into 1-inch cubes

3 pounds hard-shell (littleneck) clams, cockles, or mussels, well washed

1 to 1½ pounds shrimp or scallops, cut into bite-size pieces if necessary

1 to 1½ pounds cod or other delicate white-fleshed fish, cut into 6 large chunks

1 tablespoon minced garlic

1 cup roughly chopped fresh parsley

1. Put the olive oil in a casserole or large saucepan over medium heat. Add the onions and cook, stirring occasionally, until softened, about 5 minutes. Meanwhile, use a vegetable peeler to strip the zest from

the oranges (save the oranges themselves for another use). Add the zest, fennel, saffron, if you're using it, and chile and cook for about a minute. Add the tomatoes and turn the heat to medium-high. When the mixture boils, reduce the heat to medium and cook, stirring occasionally, until the mixture becomes saucelike, 10 to 15 minutes. (You can prepare the dish several hours in advance up to this point; cover and set aside until you're ready to eat.)

2. Add the monkfish and raise the heat to medium-high. When the mixture begins to boil, reduce the heat to medium-low and cook, stirring occasionally, until it is just about tender, 10 minutes or so.

3. Add the clams, raise the heat to high, and stir; when the mixture boils, reduce the heat to low, cover, and cook until the clams begin to open, 5 to 10 minutes. (Any clams that do not open can be pried open at the table with a butter knife.) Add the shrimp and cod, stir, and cover; cook, stirring gently once or twice, until the cod is almost done (a thin-bladed knife will pierce it with little resistance), about 5 minutes. (If the mixture is very thick—there should be some broth—add a cup or so of hot water.) Stir in the garlic and cook 1 minute more. Stir in the parsley and serve with crusty bread.

Wine: Rosé or a light red

Serving: Chile-Fried Shrimp with Scallions and Orange (page 30), 60-Minute Bread (Pizza, Pasta & Grains, page 72), Simple Green Salad (Vegetables, page 10)

Paella, Fast and Easy

Although you wouldn't know it from the massive dish served in restaurants, paella has simple roots. The word itself comes not from a fancy combination of rice, seafood, sausage, and meat, but from *paellera*, a large pan that looks like a flat wok. And the only ingredient common to every traditional paella is rice—which makes sense, since the dish originated in Valencia, Spain's great rice-growing region.

Some people argue that a true paella must contain only meat or seafood, never both, that a true paella can be prepared only in a *paellera*, or that true paella must be cooked outdoors over wood. Perhaps they're all right. What's clear to me is that you can produce a fabulous rice dish I call paella in just over half an hour, which makes it a great option for weeknights.

Makes: 4 servings

Time: 30 minutes

---

4 cups chicken stock

Pinch of saffron (optional)

3 tablespoons extra virgin olive oil

1 medium onion, peeled and minced

2 cups medium-grain rice

Salt and freshly ground black pepper

2 cups peeled shrimp, cut into ½-inch chunks

Minced fresh parsley

1. Preheat the oven to 500°F, or as near that temperature as you can get it. Warm the stock in a saucepan along with the saffron if you're using it. Place an ovenproof 10- or 12-inch skillet over medium-high heat and pour in the oil. A minute later, add the onion and cook, stirring occasionally, until translucent, about 5 minutes.

2. Add the rice and cook, stirring occasionally, until glossy, just a minute or two. Season liberally with salt and pepper and add the warmed stock, taking care to avoid the rising steam. Stir in the shrimp and transfer the skillet to the oven.

3. Bake for about 25 minutes, until all the liquid is absorbed and the rice is dry on top. Garnish with parsley and serve immediately.

Wine: Albariño, the great Spanish white, would be ideal. A light red wouldn't be bad either.

Serving: You need nothing more than a salad or a simple vegetable dish. A little bread doesn't hurt. And if you're feeling ambitious, Piquillo Peppers with Shiitakes and Spinach (Vegetables, page 52).

Poultry

Chicken Curry with Coconut Milk

Coconut milk could hardly be easier to use. Like canned tomatoes, it is the foundation of certain essential dishes, especially those of India, Southeast Asia, and the Caribbean. Like canned chicken stock, it can turn a dry dish into a pleasantly saucy one in about two minutes. Like both, it can be always there for you, since it is also sold in cans. This dish, a simple, fast curry, is made sweet and creamy by nothing more than the addition of coconut milk; it's a snap.

Makes: 4 servings

Time: 30 to 40 minutes

---

2 tablespoons vegetable oil

2 large onions, sliced

Salt and freshly ground black pepper

2 teaspoons curry powder

One 12- to 14-ounce can (1½ to 2 cups) unsweetened coconut milk

1½ pounds boneless, skinless chicken, cut into ¾- to 1-inch chunks

1 cup peeled, seeded, and diced tomato (canned is fine; cut up and drain before using)

Chopped fresh basil or mint

1. Pour the oil into a large skillet, turn the heat to medium-high, and heat for a minute. Add the onions along with a generous pinch of salt and some pepper. Reduce the heat to medium and cook, stirring occasionally, until the onions are very soft and almost falling apart, 15 minutes or more. Raise the heat again and brown them a bit, then stir in the curry powder and cook, stirring, for another minute or so.

2. Reduce the heat to medium, add the coconut milk, and cook, stirring occasionally, until it thickens, about 2 minutes. Add the chicken and stir, then cook until done, 3 to 6 minutes. (If you're in doubt whether the chicken is done, cut into a piece.)

3. Add the tomato and cook for another minute; taste and adjust the seasoning as necessary. Garnish with basil and serve.

Wine: Dry Riesling or Gewürztraminer or beer

Serving: White or brown rice, or any rice dish; Herbed Green Salad with Soy Vinaigrette (Vegetables, page 12) or any light salad

Chicken Breasts with Eggplant, Shallots, and Ginger

Eggplant is so strongly associated with the cooking of Italy and southern France that regardless of cooking method, it is almost always prepared with olive oil and garlic. This need not be the case, of course, and with a few ingredient changes—like the addition of ginger—you can make a novel and delicious kind of "ratatouille" that readily converts an ordinary grilled or broiled boneless chicken breast into an unusual and appealing dish.

Makes: 4 servings

Time: 30 to 40 minutes

8 ounces shallots (about 6 large)

¼ cup grapeseed, corn, or other light oil

1 to 1¼ pounds eggplant, cut into 1-inch cubes

Salt and freshly ground black pepper

2 tablespoons peeled, minced fresh ginger, or 2 teaspoons dried

1½ pounds boneless, skinless chicken breasts (4 half breasts)

¼ cup minced fresh cilantro, or more to taste

1. Peel the shallots and cut them in half the long way (most large shallots have two lobes anyway, and will naturally divide in half as you peel them). If they are small, peel them and leave them whole. Start a

medium-hot charcoal or wood fire, preheat a gas grill to the maximum, or preheat the broiler. Set the rack 4 inches from the heat source.

2. Pour the oil into a large nonstick skillet and turn the heat to medium-high. Add the shallots and cook for about 5 minutes, stirring occasionally, until they begin to brown. Add the eggplant, salt, and pepper and lower the heat to medium. Cook, stirring occasionally, until the eggplant softens, about 15 minutes.

3. When the eggplant begins to brown, add 1 tablespoon of the ginger and cook for another 3 minutes or so, until the eggplant is very tender and the mixture fragrant. Meanwhile, rub the chicken breasts with salt, pepper, and the remaining 1 tablespoon of the ginger. Grill or broil for 3 minutes per side, or until done.

4. Stir 2 tablespoons of the cilantro into the eggplant mixture. Serve the chicken breasts on a bed of the eggplant and garnish with the remaining 2 tablespoons cilantro.

Wine: Rough red from the south of France, Zinfandel, Syrah, or Chianti

Serving: 60-Minute Bread (Pizza, Pasta & Grains, page 72) or good store-bought bread; boiled potatoes or Mashed Potatoes (Vegetables, page 74)

Steamed Chicken Breasts with Scallion-Ginger Sauce

This Chinese dipping sauce is served with chicken that has been steamed, then lightly dressed with soy and sesame oil.

Makes: 4 servings

Time: 20 to 30 minutes

---

4 chicken breast halves, bone-in or boneless

1 tablespoon peeled, minced fresh ginger

½ cup grapeseed, corn, or other light oil

¼ cup trimmed and chopped scallions, both white and green parts (¼-inch pieces)

Salt

2 tablespoons good soy sauce

1 teaspoon toasted sesame oil

1. Steam the chicken over simmering water for 6 to 10 minutes for boneless breasts, 10 to 15 minutes for bone-in. The chicken is done when white and firm to the touch; cut into a piece if you want to be certain.

2. Stir together the ginger, oil, scallions, and salt to taste in a bowl. The mixture should be quite strong; you can add more ginger, scallions, or salt if you like.

3. When the chicken is done, drizzle it with the soy sauce and sesame oil. Pass the sauce at the table or divide it among 4 small bowls for dipping.

Wine: Beer or a light, crisp white, like Sauvignon Blanc, Graves, Pinot Grigio, Pinot Gris, or dry Pinot Blanc

Serving: White or brown rice, or Rice Salad with Peas and Soy (Pizza, Pasta & Grains, page 86); Herbed Green Salad with Soy Vinaigrette (Vegetables, page 12).

Fastest Roast Chicken

Here it is: fast, nearly foolproof roast chicken.

Makes: 4 servings

Time: 45 to 60 minutes

---

1 chicken (3 to 4 pounds)

Salt and freshly ground black pepper

1. Preheat the oven to 450°F. Five minutes after turning on the oven, place a cast-iron or other heavy, ovenproof skillet on a rack set low in the oven. (Alternatively, put the skillet over high heat for about 3 minutes before the oven is hot.) Season the chicken with salt and pepper.

2. When the oven is hot, about 10 minutes later, carefully place the chicken, breast side up, in the hot skillet. Roast, undisturbed, for 30 minutes, or until an instant-read thermometer inserted in the meaty part of the thigh registers 155°F. Remove from the oven, let rest for a minute or two, then carve and serve.

Wine: The best red you can lay your hands on

Serving: 60-Minute Bread (Pizza, Pasta & Grains, page 72) or good store-bought bread; Mashed Potatoes (Vegetables, page 74); Steamed Broccoli with a Beurre Noisette (Vegetables, page 32); Glazed Carrots (Vegetables, page 61)

Broiled Cornish Hens with Lemon and Balsamic Vinegar

All sourness is not the same, as this simple preparation of broiled Cornish hens with lemon and vinegar demonstrates. I wanted to develop a dish that would take advantage of the complex flavor of the entire lemon, rind and all, and offset it with another equally gentle sourness.

The result is a crisp-skinned Cornish hen (you could use chicken, of course), topped with nicely browned lemon slices (sweet and tender enough to eat) and drizzled with just enough balsamic vinegar to make you wonder where the extra flavor is coming from. A garnish of parsley or a hint of rosemary and garlic make nice additions.

Makes: 4 servings

Time: 30 to 40 minutes

---

2 Cornish hens or 1 3- to 4-pound chicken

Salt and freshly ground black pepper

2 lemons

2 teaspoons balsamic vinegar, or to taste

Chopped fresh parsley

1. Preheat the broiler and adjust the rack so that it is about 4 inches from the heat source. Use a sharp, sturdy knife to split the hens through their backbones; it will cut through without too much effort. Flatten the

hens in a broiling or roasting pan, skin side down, and liberally sprinkle the exposed surfaces with salt and pepper. Slice one of the lemons as thinly as you can and lay the slices on the birds.

2. Broil for about 10 minutes, or until the lemon is browned and the birds appear cooked on this side; rotate the pan in the oven if necessary. Turn the birds, sprinkle with salt and pepper, and return to the broiler. Cook for another 10 minutes, or until the skin of the birds is nicely browned. Meanwhile, slice the remaining lemon as you did the first.

3. Lay the lemon slices on the birds' skin side and return to the broiler. Broil for another 5 minutes, by which time the lemons will be slightly browned and the meat cooked through; if it isn't, broil for an additional couple of minutes. If you are cooking a whole chicken, make sure the internal temperature reaches 165°F before removing from the oven. Drizzle with the balsamic vinegar, garnish with parsley, and serve.

Wine: Rosé from Provence or the Rhône, lightly chilled, or a light red like a Beaujolais

Serving: 60-Minute Bread (Pizza, Pasta & Grains, page 72) or good store-bought bread; white or brown rice, or Mashed Potatoes (Vegetables, page 74); Steamed Broccoli with a Beurre Noisette (Vegetables, page 32)

Chicken Thighs with Mexican Flavors

The dark, rich meat of a chicken thigh responds brilliantly to the strong, equatorial flavors most closely associated with grilling. This Mexican-style treatment packs plenty of punch, even if you use the minimum amount of cayenne (as I do), or omit it entirely.

Makes: 8 servings

Time: 30 to 60 minutes

8 garlic cloves

1 large onion, quartered

2 tablespoons fresh oregano leaves, or 1 teaspoon dried

1 tablespoon ground cumin

½ teaspoon cayenne, or to taste

Pinch of ground cloves

Salt and freshly ground black pepper

2 tablespoons peanut or other oil

¼ cup orange juice, preferably freshly squeezed

¼ cup fresh lime juice

About 3 pounds boneless chicken thighs, or 4 pounds bone-in thighs

Minced fresh cilantro

1. Preheat a gas grill or start a wood or charcoal fire, or preheat the broiler; the fire should be moderately hot, and the rack at least 4 inches from the heat source. Combine the garlic, onion, oregano, cumin, cayenne, cloves, salt, pepper, and oil in a blender or small food processor and blend until fairly smooth. Add the juices, then taste and adjust the seasoning; the blend should be powerful.

2. Smear this mixture all over the chicken; if time allows, marinate the chicken for 30 minutes or so. Grill or broil 6 to 8 minutes per side, watching carefully, until the meat is nicely browned on the outside and cooked through on the inside (bone-in thighs will take longer, about 20 minutes total). Serve hot or at room temperature, garnished with the cilantro.

Wine: A simple, crisp, inexpensive white—Muscadet, Graves, or Pinot Grigio, for example—will do well here, but so will good beer.

Serving: Scallop Seviche (Small Plates & Soups, page 28), Herbed Green Salad with Nut Vinaigrette (Vegetables, page 11)

Chicken with Pancetta and Balsamic Vinegar

A simple dish that is made special by real Italian ingredients.

Makes: 8 servings

Time: 45 minutes

2 tablespoons extra virgin olive oil

¼ pound pancetta, cut into bits

2 chickens, about 3 pounds each, cut into serving pieces, or 8 legs, cut in two, or 16 thighs

Salt and freshly ground black pepper

16 garlic cloves, peeled and left whole

1½ cups white wine or water

¼ cup balsamic vinegar

Minced fresh parsley (optional)

1. Preheat the oven to 400°F. Put the oil in a large skillet, preferably nonstick, and turn the heat to medium-high. A minute later, add about half the pancetta and cook, stirring occasionally, until it begins to give up some of its fat, just a minute or so. Add as much chicken as will fit comfortably (probably about half), skin side down. Season with salt and pepper and scatter half the garlic in the pan. Quickly brown the chicken on both sides—no more than 10 minutes total—then transfer it, skin side up, to a roasting pan. Repeat the process, adding more oil to the skillet if necessary, and transferring the second batch to the same roasting pan. Put the pan in the oven.

2. While the chicken is roasting, make the sauce: Pour off all but 2 tablespoons of fat from the pan. Add the wine and raise the heat to high. Cook, stirring occasionally and scraping the bottom of the pan if necessary to loosen any browned bits that are stuck there. When the sauce is very thick and glossy, barely covering the bottom of the pan, turn off the heat and stir in the vinegar. When the chicken is cooked through (about 20 minutes; cut into a piece or two if necessary to check), spoon the sauce (including all the pancetta and garlic) over the chicken, garnish with parsley, if you like, and serve.

Wine: Chianti, or any other fruity but gutsy red, like Zinfandel or a Côtes du Rhône

Serving: 60-Minute Bread (Pizza, Pasta & Grains, page 72), Porcini-Scented "Wild" Mushroom Sauté (Vegetables, page 76), Simple Green Salad (Vegetables, page 10)

Coq au Vin with Prunes

The chicken must be well browned before proceeding with the dish, and in this instance there is no hurrying the process. Take your time and brown each piece well; this will take a while, especially if you're cooking for eight or more, as you'll have to brown in batches.

Makes: 8 servings

Time: 1 hour

---

2 tablespoons olive oil

2 chickens (3 to 4 pounds each), cut into serving pieces

Salt and freshly ground black pepper

2 large onions, chopped

½ cup minced salt pork or bacon (optional)

1 tablespoon minced garlic

1½ pounds pitted prunes

1 bottle Burgundy, Pinot Noir, or other fruity red wine

4 tablespoons (½ stick) unsalted butter (optional)

Minced fresh parsley

1. Put the oil in a large skillet, preferably nonstick, and turn the heat to medium-high. A minute later, add as many of the chicken pieces as will fit without crowding, skin side down. Cook, rotating the pieces and adjusting the heat as necessary to cook them evenly, until nicely browned on the skin side, about 5 minutes; turn and brown on the other side(s). As the pieces are done, sprinkle them with salt and

pepper, transfer them to a large flameproof casserole, and add the remaining pieces to the pan.

2. When all the chicken is browned, add the onions to the fat remaining in the skillet; cook over medium-high heat, stirring occasionally, until softened, 5 minutes or so, then transfer them to the casserole. Add the salt pork, if you're using it, and cook, stirring occasionally, until brown and crisp, about 5 minutes; transfer to the casserole and drain all but 1 tablespoon of the fat. Turn the heat to medium and add the garlic and, 30 seconds later, the prunes. Cook for a minute, stirring once or twice, then add to the casserole.

3. Turn the heat under the skillet to high and add half the wine. Cook, stirring and scraping the bottom of the pan to loosen any solid particles there, until the wine is reduced by half. Pour into the casserole along with the remaining wine. Turn the heat under the casserole to high and bring to a boil; stir, then reduce the heat to low and cover. Simmer, stirring once or twice, until the chicken is done, about 30 minutes. Remove the top, stir in the optional butter, and raise the heat to high; cook until the sauce thickens a bit. Taste and adjust the seasoning if necessary; garnish with parsley and serve.

Wine: The best red you can find—a great Burgundy would not be out of place here.

Serving: 60-Minute Bread (Pizza, Pasta & Grains, page 72), Roasted Asparagus with Parmesan (Vegetables, page 45)

Roast Duck in One Hour

What turns people off to roasting duck—its thick layer of subcutaneous fat—is actually its best feature, one that makes it a nearly foolproof dish, absolutely suitable for a weeknight meal. The fat keeps the meat juicy even when it's well done—a distinct advantage because the breast is best medium-rare, but the legs must be cooked through, or nearly so, to be palatable.

In fact, duck is so difficult to roast badly that all experienced cooks seem to claim their procedure is the best. Having tried many methods, I can say that the results are all about the same. So I usually rely on the one presented here, which I believe is the easiest way to guarantee a succulent but beautifully browned bird.

Makes: 2 to 4 servings

Time: About 1 hour

One 4- to 5-pound duck

Freshly ground black pepper

½ cup soy sauce, more or less

1. Preheat the oven to 450°F. Discard the neck and giblets or keep them for another use; remove excess fat from the duck's cavity.

2. Place the duck, breast side down (wings up), on a rack in a roasting pan; add water to come to just below the rack. Sprinkle with pepper and brush with a little soy sauce.

3. Roast for 30 minutes, undisturbed. Prick the back all over with the point of a sharp knife, then flip the bird onto its back. Sprinkle with pepper and brush with soy sauce again. Add a little more water to the bottom of the pan if the juices are spattering (do this carefully—you don't want to get water on the duck).

4. Roast 20 minutes, prick the breast all over with the point of a knife, and brush with soy sauce. Roast 10 minutes; brush with soy sauce. Roast another 5 or 10 minutes if necessary, until the duck is a glorious brown all over and an instant-read thermometer inserted into the thigh measures at least 155°F. Let rest for 5 minutes before carving and serving.

Wine: Roast duck can stand up well to a good red wine, from a rich red to something soft like Rioja.

Serving: An assortment of lightly cooked vegetables is ideal, along with potatoes however you like them.

Slow-Cooked Duck Legs with Olives

Unless you've made your own duck confit, you may never have cooked duck legs by themselves; but in many ways they're superior to both duck breasts and whole birds. They're quite lean, and just a quick trimming of the excess fat is all that's necessary. Given proper cooking—that is, long, slow cooking—they become fork-tender and richly flavorful, reminiscent of some of the "lesser" cuts of beef and pork, like brisket and cheek. Finally, it's easy enough to cook enough legs for eight—which is hardly the case with whole duck!

Makes: 8 servings

Time: 2 hours, largely unattended

---

8 duck legs

10 or more garlic cloves

2 cups olives, preferably a combination of green and black

Several thyme sprigs

One 28-ounce can tomatoes, with their juice

1 large onion, roughly chopped (optional)

2 carrots, roughly chopped (optional)

2 celery stalks, roughly chopped (optional)

Salt and freshly ground black pepper

Chopped fresh parsley

1. Trim all visible fat from the duck legs, then lay them in a large, broad skillet; they can overlap if necessary. Turn the heat to medium and add the garlic, olives, thyme, and tomatoes. Add the onion, carrots, and celery, if using. Season with salt and pepper. When the mixture reaches a lively simmer, turn the heat to low and cover.

2. Cook, checking occasionally—the mixture should be gently bubbling when you remove the cover—until the duck is very tender, about 1½ hours. Transfer the duck to a warm plate and cover (or place in a very low oven), then turn the heat to medium-high under the remaining sauce. Cook, stirring occasionally, until the mixture is reduced to a thick, saucelike consistency, about 10 minutes. Spoon over the duck legs, garnish with the chopped parsley, and serve.

Wine: Red, for sure, preferably something rich and wonderful. A classified Bordeaux or cru bourgeois would not be out of place; good California Cabernet would also be wonderful.

Serving: Prosciutto, Fig, and Parmesan Rolls (Small Plates & Soups, page 8); 60-Minute Bread (Pizza, Pasta & Grains, page 72), Raw Beet Salad (Vegetables, page 27)

Braised Goose with Pears or Apples

Any dried fruit can be used in this preparation, but dried pears and dried apples hold their shape better and are a little less sweet than prunes and apricots; there's no reason you can't substitute, however, or combine.

Makes: 6 servings

Time: About 3 hours, largely unattended

1 goose, cut into serving pieces, excess fat removed

Salt and freshly ground black pepper

½ cup diced bacon or pancetta (optional)

2 large onions, roughly chopped

4 bay leaves

A few thyme sprigs

½ pound dried pears or apples

2 cups dry white wine

1 tablespoon white wine, Champagne, or sherry vinegar

About 2 pounds pears or apples, peeled, cored, and sliced

1. Turn the heat to medium-high under a casserole or deep skillet at least 12 inches across; a minute later, add the goose pieces, skin side down. Cook, rearranging the pieces now and then so that they brown evenly, until nicely browned and rendered of fat, 10 to 15 minutes. Sprinkle

with salt and pepper and turn; brown 2 or 3 minutes on the meat side. Remove the goose and pour off all but a tablespoon of the fat.

2. If you're using it, cook the bacon in the same skillet over medium-high heat until brown and crisp all over, about 10 minutes. Add the onions, bay leaves, and thyme. Cook, stirring occasionally and seasoning with more salt and pepper, until the onions are softened, about 10 minutes. Add the dried fruit and cook another minute or two, stirring occasionally. Add the wine and raise the heat to high; cook until the wine is reduced by about half, 5 minutes or so.

3. Return the goose pieces to the skillet and turn the heat to very low. Cover and cook (the mixture should be bubbling, but barely) for at least 2 hours, turning only once or twice, until the goose is very tender. Add the vinegar, sliced fresh fruit, and a good grinding of black pepper; cover and cook, stirring occasionally, until the fruit is tender, 10 to 15 minutes. Remove and discard the bay leaves and thyme sprigs. Taste, adjust the seasoning, and serve.

Wine: The best option is a good Pinot Noir (red Burgundy); Cabernet Sauvignon (red Bordeaux) would be a close second.

Serving: Roast New Potatoes with Rosemary (Vegetables, page 67), Herbed Green Salad with Nut Vinaigrette (Vegetables, page 11)

Meat

Skirt Steak with Plum Puree Sauce

This is an enriched, slightly sour puree of fresh plums that complements steak brilliantly.

Makes: 4 servings

Time: 40 to 50 minutes

---

3 tablespoons unsalted butter

1 cup Plum Puree (recipe follows)

About 1½ pounds skirt steak, cut into 4 portions

Salt and freshly ground black pepper

⅛ teaspoon cayenne, or to taste

1 tablespoon fresh lemon juice

2 tablespoons minced fresh parsley

1. Prepare a gas or charcoal grill; the fire should be extremely hot. (You can broil or pan-grill the steak if you prefer.) Meanwhile, place the butter in a small saucepan and turn the heat to medium. Cook, shaking the pan occasionally, until the butter turns light brown, about 5 minutes. Lower the heat and stir in the purée. Cook, stirring, for about a minute; keep warm.

2. When the fire is ready, grill the steak, 2 minutes per side for rare, 1 to 2 minutes longer for medium-rare to medium. Season the steak with salt and pepper as it cooks.

3. While the steak cooks add the cayenne, lemon juice, and a pinch of salt to the puree and stir; taste and adjust the seasoning. Serve the steak with the sauce, garnished with the parsley.

Plum Puree

About 1 pound fresh plums

1. To peel, plunge the plums into boiling water for about 30 seconds, or until the skin loosens; then immerse them into ice water to stop the cooking. Remove the skins with a paring knife. Then cut the fruit into halves or quarters and remove the pits. Generally, a pound of fruit will produce just over a cup of puree.

2. To puree, cram the plums into the blender, pushing them down onto the blades and squeezing some of the water from them. This should make it easy to puree the fruit without any intervention or added liquid. If the machine is having trouble, turn it off and use a wooden spoon or rubber spatula to mash the fruit down onto the blades.

3. The puree is stable, but its flavor is fleeting and will become less intense with every hour. If you are not ready to proceed after making it, refrigerate in a tightly covered container and use within a day.

Wine: Rioja or another soft, lush red

Serving: Roasted Red Peppers (Vegetables, page 58) and/or Simple Green Salad (Vegetables, page 10)

Grilled Steaks with Roquefort Sauce

It may be that the paradigm of steak-and-cheese combinations is the Philly cheese steak, but there is a more elegant and arguably better-tasting way to combine these two foods: Top steak with a simple sauce based on blue cheese. This dish, which often appears on bistro menus in France, fits the need for a good steak served with something powerfully salty and rich (anchovy butter, or a combination of butter, soy sauce, and ginger also does the trick). Some might consider the sauce overkill, but not those of us who crave it.

Makes: 4 servings

Time: 30 to 40 minutes

---

1 tablespoon unsalted butter or grapeseed, corn, or other light oil

¼ cup minced shallots

2 tablespoons white wine vinegar or cider vinegar

6 ounces Roquefort or other blue cheese, crumbled

Generous pinch of cayenne

Salt

1½ to 2 pounds strip steaks, filet mignon, or rib-eye steaks

Minced fresh parsley or chives (optional)

1. Start a hot charcoal or wood fire, preheat a gas grill to the maximum, or preheat the broiler. The fire should be quite hot, and the grill rack no more than 4 inches from the heat source.

2. Put the butter in a small saucepan and turn the heat to medium. When the butter melts and its foam begins to subside, add the shallots and cook until soft, stirring occasionally, about 5 minutes. Add the vinegar, stir, and cook until it is just about evaporated, 1 to 2 minutes. Turn the heat to low and stir in the cheese and cayenne. Stir occasionally until the cheese melts, then taste and adjust the seasoning as necessary (it's unlikely that the sauce will need any salt). Keep warm while you grill the steaks.

3. Season the steaks well with salt, then grill or broil for 3 to 4 minutes per side for medium-rare, or longer or shorter according to your taste. Cut into four portions and serve the steaks with a spoonful or two of sauce ladled over each, garnished with parsley, if you like.

Wine: Rioja, Dolcetto, or another red from Spain or Northern Italy

Serving: Simple Green Salad (Vegetables, page 10) or Tomato Salad with Basil (Vegetables, page 20); Mashed Potatoes (Vegetables, page 74) or Pan-Crisped Potatoes (Vegetables, page 68); Steamed Broccoli with a Beurre Noisette (Vegetables, page 32)

Roast Sirloin of Beef

Few meats are as tender, juicy, and flavorful as roast beef, yet none is easier to prepare, given the appropriate cut and proper technique. Two of the best cuts for roasting, filet (or tenderloin) and standing rib, are not always ideal. The first is supremely tender, but expensive and nearly tasteless; the second tends to be sold in large cuts that are too unwieldy for most weeknights. But the sirloin strip, also called New York strip—the same cut that makes for some of the best steaks—is perfect when cut in a single large piece. Ask your butcher for a 2- or 3-pound piece of sirloin strip—essentially a steak cut as a roast—and you should have it within minutes.

Makes: 4 to 6 servings

Time: 50 to 60 minutes

One 2½- to 3-pound piece sirloin strip

Salt and freshly ground black pepper

1. Preheat the oven to 500°F. Set a skillet large enough to hold the roast in the oven so it preheats as well. Sprinkle the meat liberally with salt and pepper.

2. When the oven and pan are hot, add the roast to the pan, top (fatty) side down, and roast for 10 minutes. Turn and roast fatty side up for 10 more minutes. Turn and roast for 5 minutes, then turn again and roast for 5 minutes. Total cooking time is 30 minutes.

3. At this point the roast will be nicely browned all over. When a meat thermometer inserted into the center of the meat, about 1 inch from one of the ends, registers 120°F, the meat will be rare to medium-rare. Cook longer if you like, but beware that from this point on it will increase a stage of doneness every 3 to 5 minutes.

4. Let the roast rest for 5 to 10 minutes, then carve and serve with its juices.

Wine: Good Bordeaux or Burgundy, or decent Rioja

Serving: 60-Minute Bread (Pizza, Pasta & Grains, page 72) or good store-bought bread, Tomato Salad with Basil (Vegetables, page 20) or Simple Green Salad (Vegetables, page 10), Mashed Potatoes (Vegetables, page 74) or Pan-Crisped Potatoes (Vegetables, page 68, Steamed Broccoli with a Beurre Noisette (Vegetables, page 32)

Pot Roast
with Cranberries

Unlike their cousin, blueberries—which are sometimes used in savory cooking, although almost never successfully—cranberries are not at all sweet, and so make a much more natural companion for meat.

Makes: 4 to 6 servings

Time: 2 hours, or more

1 tablespoon unsalted butter or extra virgin olive oil

½ cup sugar

One 2- to 3-pound piece chuck or brisket

Salt and freshly ground black pepper

½ cup sherry vinegar or good wine vinegar

12 ounces fresh or frozen cranberries

1 orange

Cayenne

1. Put the butter in a flameproof casserole or skillet and turn the heat to medium-high. Put the sugar on a plate and dredge the meat in it until all surfaces are coated. Reserve the remaining sugar. When the butter foam subsides, brown the meat on all sides—this will take about 15 minutes—seasoning it with salt and pepper as it browns.

2. When the meat is nicely browned, add the vinegar and cook for a minute, stirring. Add the cranberries and remaining sugar and stir. Strip the zest from the orange (you can do it in broad strips, with a small knife or vegetable peeler) and add it to the skillet. Juice the orange and add the juice also, along with a pinch of cayenne. Turn the heat to low and cover; the mixture should bubble but not furiously.

3. Cook, turning the meat and stirring every 30 minutes, for 2 hours or longer, or until the meat is tender. When the meat is done, taste and adjust the seasoning if necessary. Turn off the heat and let the roast rest for a few minutes, then carve and serve with the sauce.

Wine: Rioja, Merlot, or another soft red

Serving: 60-Minute Bread (Pizza, Pasta & Grains, page 72) or good store-bought bread; Steamed Broccoli with a Beurre Noisette (Vegetables, page 32) or Glazed Carrots (Vegetables, page 61); Mashed Potatoes (Vegetables, page 74) or Pan-Crisped Potatoes (Vegetables, page 68)

Beef with Caramelized Sugar

Caramel is the key to what makes this dish distinctive; though it is made from sugar, it gains a certain bitterness if you cook it long enough. Chances are no one will be able to figure out how you made this.

Makes: 8 servings

Time: 2 hours or less

One 4-pound piece boneless chuck roast

2 large onions, sliced

Salt and freshly ground black pepper

2 cups stock or water

2 cups sugar

2 lemons

2 tablespoons soy sauce

1. Heat a large, deep skillet over medium-high heat for a couple of minutes, then add the beef. Sear on one side until nicely browned, about 5 minutes, then sear on the other side. Transfer to a plate, turn the heat to medium, and add the onions. Season them with salt and pepper and cook, stirring occasionally, until tender, 5 to 10 minutes.

2. Return the meat to the pan and season it with more salt and pepper; add the stock, bring to a boil, turn the heat to low, and cover the pan. It should bubble steadily but not vigorously. Cook until the meat is tender, at least an hour.

3. When the meat is done, put the sugar in a small, heavy saucepan over medium-high heat; add a couple tablespoons of water. Cook, shaking the pan occasionally, until the sugar melts and turns dark golden brown. Carefully add about half the caramel to the simmering beef and stir. Slice one of the lemons and add it, along with the soy sauce. If the mixture is appealingly salty and bitter, it is done; if it is tame, add more salt, pepper, and/or some of the caramel (discard the remaining caramel). Juice the remaining lemon and add the juice, to taste, to the sauce. Carve the meat and serve it with the sauce.

Wine: Serve a fruity Riesling, very cold, or a not-too-dry rosé, also chilled. Or good beer.

Serving: White or brown rice, Seaweed Salad with Cucumber (Vegetables, page 22)

Osso Buco

There is no promise of speed here: Osso buco takes time. But this classic Italian dish of glorious, marrow-filled veal shanks (the name means "bone with hole"), braised until they are fork-tender, is dead easy to make and requires a total of no more than fifteen or twenty minutes of attention during its two hours or so of cooking. And it holds well enough overnight so that 90 percent of the process can be accomplished while you're watching television the night before you serve the dish.

Makes: 4 servings

Time: At least 2 hours, largely unattended

---

1 tablespoon extra virgin olive oil

4 center-cut slices veal shank, 2 pounds or more

Salt and freshly ground black pepper

3 or 4 garlic cloves, lightly smashed and peeled

4 anchovy fillets

1 cup dry white wine, chicken or beef stock, or water

2 teaspoons unsalted butter (optional)

1. Heat a large, deep skillet over medium-high heat for a couple of minutes. Add the oil, swirl it around, and pour out any excess. Add the veal and cook until nicely browned on the first side (for even browning, you can rotate the shanks, but try not to disturb them too much), about 5 minutes. Turn and brown the other side.

2. When the second side is just about completely browned, sprinkle the shanks with a little salt and pepper and add the garlic and anchovies to the pan. Cook, stirring a little, until the anchovies dissolve and the garlic browns, about 2 minutes. Add the liquid and let it bubble away for about a minute.

3. Turn the heat to low and cover the skillet. Five minutes later, check to see that the mixture is simmering—just a few bubbles appearing at once—and adjust the heat accordingly. Cook until the meat is very tender and pulling away from the bone, at least 90 minutes and probably somewhat more; turn the veal every half hour or so. (When the meat is tender you may turn off the heat and refrigerate the dish for up to 24 hours; reheat gently before proceeding.)

4. Transfer the meat to a warm platter and turn the heat to high. Boil the sauce until it becomes thick and glossy, about 5 minutes. Stir in the butter if you like and serve the meat with the sauce spooned over it.

Wine: A rich, good red like Barolo, a not-too-dry Cabernet, or a Rioja

Serving: The traditional accompaniment is risotto with Parmesan (risotto alla Milanese), and you cannot do much better, though Parmesan Cups with Orzo Risotto (Small Plates & Soups, page 12) are great (even without the cups). For some reason, I also love cooked carrots with osso buco.

Crisp Roasted Rack of Lamb

Rack of lamb—a row of unseparated rib chops—has been a restaurant feature for so long that many people assume there is some trick to cooking it. But there is not. You trim the rack of excess fat and roast it at high heat. Salt and pepper are good seasonings, there are a number of quick tricks for adding flavor to the exterior, and you can, of course, make a quick reduction sauce before serving it. But these are options and by my standards unnecessary: The distinctive flavor of true lamb is an uncommonly fine treat.

Makes: 4 servings

Time: 30 minutes

2 racks of lamb, each about 1½ pounds

Salt and freshly ground black pepper

1. Preheat the oven to 500°F. Strip most of the surface fat from the lamb (your butcher may already have done this). Cut between the ribs, almost down to the meaty eye. Divide each rack in half down the middle, sprinkle with salt and pepper to taste, and place in a roasting pan.

2. Roast for 15 minutes, then insert a meat thermometer straight in from one end into the meatiest part. If it reads 125°F or more, remove the lamb immediately. If it reads 120°F or less, put the lamb back for about 5 minutes. Remove and let sit for 5 minutes; this will give you medium- to medium-rare lamb on the outer ribs, medium-rare to rare in the center. Cook a little longer for more doneness if you prefer. Serve, separating the ribs by cutting down straight through them.

Wine: Break out the best red you have: Bordeaux or other good Cabernet is the classic.

Serving: Crisp potatoes, whether roasted or sautéed, are ideal. An elegant vegetable gratin would be great (see, for example, Roasted Asparagus with Parmesan, Vegetables, page 45), but so would a simply steamed vegetable or a salad.

Lamb with Peaches

A logical combination, and glorious once you taste it, with the sweet juice of the peaches deftly cutting through the richness of the lamb without being piercing. A hint of cinnamon (or an even smaller one of allspice—maybe ⅛ teaspoon) gives the dish a great aroma as it cooks and a slightly mysterious flavor at the table. A pinch of cayenne or other red pepper makes a nice addition.

Makes: 4 servings

Time: About 1½ hours, largely unattended

---

2 pounds boned lamb shoulder, trimmed of fat and gristle and cut into 1- to 1½-inch pieces

Salt

1 cinnamon stick or ½ teaspoon ground cinnamon

¼ teaspoon cayenne or other red pepper to taste

1 medium to large onion, cut in half

½ cup Port wine, red wine, or water

4 medium to large ripe peaches

Juice of 1 lemon

1 cup roughly chopped fresh parsley

1. Place the lamb in a 12-inch skillet and turn the heat to medium-high. Season with salt and add the cinnamon, cayenne, onion, and wine. Bring to a boil, cover, and adjust the heat so that the mixture simmers steadily but not violently. Cook for 1 to 1½ hours, checking and stirring every 15 minutes or so, adding a little more liquid in the unlikely event that the mixture cooks dry. (This probably means that the heat is too high; turn it down a bit.)

2. When the meat is tender when poked with a small, sharp knife, remove the onion and cinnamon stick, then turn the heat to medium-high and cook off any remaining liquid, allowing the lamb to brown a little. Cut the peaches in half and remove their pits, then cut each of them into 12 or 16 wedges. Stir in the peaches and continue to cook, gently tossing or stirring the mixture, until the peaches are glazed and quite soft but still intact, about 5 minutes.

3. Stir in the lemon juice and most of the parsley; taste and adjust the seasoning. Garnish with the remaining bit of herb and serve.

Wine: Pinot Noir or California Merlot

Serving: White or brown rice, rice pilaf, or Persian Rice with Potatoes (Pizza, Pasta & Grains, page 76); Simple Green Salad (Vegetables, page 10)

Grilled Soy-and-Ginger Boneless Leg of Lamb

Simply put, boneless lamb leg is the ideal meat for grilling. Not only is it full-flavored, it's completely forgiving; since its unusual shape virtually guarantees that some pieces will be well done while others remain rare, your guests will think you're a genius.

Makes: 8 servings

Time: About 1 hour

One 4-pound butterflied leg of lamb

1 tablespoon extra virgin olive oil

2 teaspoons salt

1 teaspoon cracked black pepper

1 tablespoon minced garlic

¼ cup soy sauce

1 tablespoon peeled and minced or grated fresh ginger

Lemon wedges

1. Start a charcoal or wood fire or preheat a gas grill or broiler; the fire should be quite hot, and the rack should be at least 4 inches from the heat source. Trim the lamb of any excess fat. Mix together the olive oil, salt, pepper, garlic, soy, and ginger; rub this mixture into the lamb well, making sure to get some into all the crevices. (The lamb may sit for an hour or more; refrigerate if it will be much longer.)

2. Grill or broil the meat until it is nicely browned, even a little charred, on both sides, 20 to 30 minutes, and the internal temperature at the thickest part is about 125°F; this will give you some lamb that is quite rare, as well as some that is nearly well done. Let rest for 5 minutes before slicing thinly, as you would a thick steak. Garnish with lemon wedges and serve.

Wine: Red and rustic, like Zinfandel, Chianti, or lightly chilled Beaujolais. A cool Provençal rosé wouldn't be bad either.

Serving: Grilled Zucchini (Vegetables, page 66), Grilled Corn (Vegetables, page 64)

Cumin-Rubbed Lamb Chops with Cucumber Salad

Lamb chops are among the best meats to grill. Although they tend to catch fire, they cook so quickly—3 minutes per side is usually more than enough—that there is no time for them to char, and the fire makes the exterior even crisper than it might be otherwise. The cucumbers are best if they're salted, which removes some of their bitterness and makes them extra crunchy.

Makes: 8 servings

Time: 1 hour, largely unattended

About 3 pounds cucumbers, peeled and thinly sliced

Salt

1 cup coarsely chopped fresh mint leaves

4 lemons

8 shoulder or leg lamb chops, or 24 rib or loin chops, about 2 pounds

Freshly ground black pepper to taste

2 tablespoons ground cumin, preferably freshly ground

1. Place the cucumber slices in a colander and sprinkle with salt, just a little more than if you were planning to eat them right away. After 15 to 30 minutes, start a charcoal or wood fire or preheat a gas grill or the broiler; the rack should be about 4 inches from the heat source.

2. When the fire is hot, press the cucumbers to extract as much liquid as possible, then toss them with the mint and the juice of one of the lemons. Rub the lamb chops with salt, pepper, and cumin and grill for about 3 minutes per side for rare, turning once.

3. Serve each of the lamb chops on a bed of the cucumber salad. Quarter the remaining lemons and serve them to squeeze over the lamb.

Wine: A rough, inexpensive type—anything from Zinfandel to chilled Beaujolais

Serving: Herbed Green Salad with Nut Vinaigrette (Vegetables, page 11), Roasted Red Peppers (Vegetables, page 58), Grilled Corn (Vegetables, page 64)

Breaded Lamb Cutlets

Though it may seem surprising, in many ways lamb is the meat most suited to this simple treatment. Like all cutlet preparations, it's lightning-quick.

Makes: 8 servings

Time: 20 minutes

Sixteen 1-inch-thick medallions of lamb, cut from 2 racks or from the loin or leg

¼ cup extra virgin olive oil

3 eggs

Panko (Japanese bread crumbs) or other bread crumbs for dredging

Salt and freshly ground black pepper

2 teaspoons ground cumin (optional), or about 1 tablespoon fresh or 1 teaspoon dried rosemary

Chopped fresh parsley (optional)

2 lemons, cut into wedges

1. Preheat the oven to 200°F. If using rib or loin slices, pound them lightly with the heel of your hand until they are about ½ inch thick. If using leg slices, put them between two pieces of wax paper or plastic wrap and pound with a mallet or rolling pin until they are about ½ inch thick. Put a nonstick or well-seasoned skillet over medium-high heat and add the oil. Beat the eggs and put the bread crumbs on a plate.

2. When the oil shimmers, dip a lamb medallion in the egg, press both sides into the bread crumbs, and add to the skillet. Do not crowd—you will have to cook in batches. When the meat is in the skillet, season it with salt and pepper and sprinkle it with a pinch of cumin or rosemary, if you like.

3. As the meat browns, flip it and brown the other side. Adjust the heat so that each side browns in about 2 minutes; the meat should remain rare. As the pieces finish, put them on a platter and keep them warm in the oven. When they are all done, garnish with parsley, if you like, and serve with lemon wedges, two medallions per serving.

Wine: Red and good. I always like Cabernet with lamb, and it can be an austere specimen from Bordeaux or a relatively fruity choice from California. Rioja would be great here, too.

Serving: Mushroom Barley Soup (Small Plates & Soups, page 60), Pilaf with Nuts and Currants (Pizza, Pasta & Grains, page 84), Tender Spinach with Crisp Shallots (Vegetables, page 39)

Slow-Cooked Lamb with Fresh Mint Sauce

Although the meat is well done, it's beyond tender (you can just about serve it with a spoon) and quite moist, especially when topped with some of the pan juices.

Makes: 8 servings

Time: About 6 hours, largely unattended

---

1 tablespoon coarse salt

4 large garlic cloves

1 whole leg of lamb, about 6 pounds, trimmed of excess fat

Freshly ground black pepper

½ cup sherry vinegar

⅓ cup sugar

2 cups fresh mint leaves

1. Preheat the oven to 250°F. Mince together the salt and garlic (if you have a small food processor, use it); with a small, sharp knife, poke holes all over the lamb and insert some of this mixture into each hole. Smear any of the remaining mixture on the lamb's skin, then sprinkle with additional salt, if necessary, and pepper. Place the lamb in a roasting pan, cover it lightly with aluminum foil, and put it in the oven. Cook for 4 hours, then remove the foil. Cook for about 2 more hours, until a sharp, thin-bladed knife can be easily inserted into the meat. If the lamb's skin is not nicely browned, raise the heat to 400°F for 10 minutes or so.

2. To make the mint sauce, combine the vinegar and sugar in a small saucepan with ⅓ cup water and a pinch of salt. Bring to a boil and cook for about 30 seconds longer. Cool for a few minutes, then combine in a blender with the mint; blend until smooth. Keep at room temperature until ready to serve (or refrigerate overnight and return to room temperature before serving).

3. Carve the lamb and spoon some of the pan juices over the slices. Serve hot, passing the mint sauce at the table.

Wine: Look for a classified Bordeaux that is at its peak, or if on a budget, go with a decent Rioja.

Serving: Green Beans and Tomatoes (Vegetables, page 28), Fast Potato Gratin (Vegetables, page 70)

Broiled Lamb Chops with Mint Chutney

Asparagus may introduce spring, but mint screams it. The perennial herb is among the first edible greens out of the ground, and it's rampant enough to be considered a weed for those who aren't fond of it. Team it with lamb, and you have a model spring dish.

Makes: 8 servings

Time: 30 minutes

Juice of 2 limes

1 garlic clove

1-inch piece of fresh ginger, peeled and roughly chopped

1 fresh or dried chile, or to taste

1 cup whole-milk yogurt

1 tablespoon sugar

2 cups chopped fresh mint leaves

Salt and freshly ground black pepper

8 shoulder lamb chops

1. Prepare a charcoal grill or preheat a gas grill or broiler; the fire should be moderately hot and the rack 4 to 6 inches from the heat source.

2. To make the chutney, combine the lime juice, garlic, ginger, chile, yogurt, and sugar in the container of a food processor or blender and puree. Stir in the mint by hand, then add salt and pepper to taste.

3. When the chutney is ready, grill the chops 3 to 4 minutes per side for medium-rare, or until they reach the desired degree of doneness. Serve the lamb chops hot, with the chutney.

Wine: Pinot Noir

Serving: Herbed Green Salad with Nut Vinaigrette (Vegetables, page 11), Mashed Potatoes (Vegetables, page 74)

Vietnamese-Style Pork

This dish has the beguiling, distinctively Southeast Asian aroma of garlic—lots of it—plus *nam pla* and lime.

Makes: 4 servings

Time: 30 to 40 minutes

2 tablespoons minced lemongrass

1 tablespoon minced garlic

3 tablespoons honey

1 tablespoon *nam pla* (Thai fish sauce), or to taste (you may substitute soy sauce)

2 limes

Freshly ground black pepper

1½ pounds country-style pork chops, preferably boneless

Chopped Thai basil, mint, cilantro, or a combination (optional)

1. Combine the lemongrass, garlic, honey, and *nam pla* in a bowl; whisk to blend. Add the juice of 1 lime and lots of pepper—about a teaspoon. Marinate the pork in this mixture while you start a charcoal or wood fire, preheat a gas grill to the maximum, or preheat a broiler; the fire should be moderately hot, and the grill rack should be about 4 inches from the heat source.

2. Grill or broil the pork, spooning the marinade over it as it cooks, until done, about 10 minutes. Turn only once, so that each side browns nicely. Serve with wedges of lime, garnished with the optional herb.

Wine: Beer, Champagne, or light Gewürztraminer

Serving: Crisp Pan-Fried Noodle Cake (Pizza, Pasta & Grains, page 62), Rice Salad with Peas and Soy (Pizza, Pasta & Grains, page 86), Herbed Green Salad with Soy Vinaigrette (Vegetables, page 12)

Slow-Cooked Ribs with Black Beans

The sauce from these ribs is fabulous with the Crisp Pan-Fried Noodle Cake (Pizza, Pasta & Grains, page 62).

Makes: 8 servings

Time: About 1½ hours

---

7 or 8 pounds spareribs, cut into 2-inch sections

2 star anise

½ cup dark soy sauce

1 cinnamon stick, about 3 inches long

½ cup mirin, or ¼ cup honey mixed with ¼ cup water

2 tablespoons sugar

2 tablespoons dry fermented black beans

1 cup dry Sherry

Minced fresh cilantro (optional)

1. Place the spareribs in a large skillet in one layer. Add the remaining ingredients except for the Sherry and cilantro, along with 1 cup water, and bring to a boil. Turn the heat to low, cover, and cook slowly—the mixture should bubble, but only gently—for at least an hour, turning the ribs every 20 minutes or so and adding more water if necessary to keep the meat from drying out.

2. When the ribs are done—the meat will be tender and practically falling off the bone—transfer them to a warm platter. Pour off most of the fat and turn the heat to high; add the Sherry (if you don't have it, water will do) and cook, scraping up any brown bits on the bottom of the pan, until the liquid is reduced by about half, about 15 minutes. Serve the ribs with this sauce over rice or the Crisp Pan-Fried Noodle Cake. Garnish with cilantro, if you like.

Wine: Beer would be preferable, but if you insist on wine, try a Gewürztraminer. Champagne is always suitable, too.

Serving: Crisp Pan-Fried Noodle Cake (Pizza, Pasta & Grains, page 62), Herbed Green Salad with Nut Vinaigrette (Vegetables, page 11)

Crispy Pork Bits with Jerk Seasonings

You'll find strongly seasoned, crunchy pork everywhere in Latin America, and it's always irresistible.

Makes: 8 servings

Time: 2 hours, largely unattended

3 pounds boneless pork shoulder, trimmed of excess fat and cut into large chunks

10 garlic cloves, crushed

2 tablespoons coriander seeds

1 dried chipotle or other chile

1 cinnamon stick

Several gratings of nutmeg

Salt

1 cup chopped fresh cilantro

4 limes, cut into wedges

1. Put the pork in a Dutch oven or deep pan; wrap the garlic, coriander, chile, and cinnamon in a piece of cheesecloth and add to the pan, along with the nutmeg and salt. Add water to cover and bring to a boil over high heat. Turn the heat to low and simmer until the pork is very tender, about 1¼ hours, adding water as necessary to keep the meat covered.

2. When the pork is tender, remove the cheesecloth sack and discard it. Raise the heat to medium-high and boil off all the liquid.

3. If you choose not to grill, you can now brown the pork in its own remaining fat. Or, thread the pork onto 8 skewers and, when you're ready to eat, grill them lightly on all sides to brown. Garnish with the cilantro and serve with the lime wedges.

Wine: Beer is most appropriate, but a chilled Pinot Noir or Beaujolais would also be terrific.

Serving: Curried Sweet Potato Soup with Apricots (Small Plates and Soups, page 64), Coconut Rice and Beans (Pizza, Pasta & Grains, page 80)

Pork Cutlets with Miso–Red Wine Sauce

In addition to its intense flavor, which is sweeter, saltier, and more complex than that of soy sauce, miso is a superb thickener, adding a rich, creamy consistency when whisked into a small amount of liquid. With that in mind, it's the work of a moment to turn the pan juices remaining after searing a piece of meat into a great sauce, using nothing more than miso and a little liquid. My choice here is pork for meat and red wine for liquid; the combination resulting from these three ingredients completely belies the amount of energy put into the dish.

Makes: 4 servings

Time: 20 minutes

Four 1-inch-thick bone-in pork chops, each about 6 ounces

Salt and freshly ground black pepper

1 cup sturdy red wine, like Zinfandel or Cabernet Sauvignon

2 tablespoons red miso

¼ cup roughly chopped fresh shiso, basil, or parsley (optional)

1. Heat a heavy skillet over medium-high heat for 2 to 3 minutes, then add the chops. Sprinkle them with a little bit of salt and a lot of pepper, then brown them on one side for 4 to 5 minutes. Turn and brown the other side until firm and nearly cooked through, another 3 or 4 minutes. Transfer to a warm plate and turn the heat to medium.

2. Add the wine and cook, stirring occasionally with a wooden spoon to loosen any bits of meat that have stuck to the pan, until the wine reduces by about half. Turn the heat to low and add the miso; stir briskly to make a smooth mixture (a wire whisk will help here).

3. Taste the sauce and add more salt (unlikely) and pepper if necessary. Spoon it over the pork, garnish with shiso if you like, and serve.

Wine: The same as, or similar to, the wine you use to make the sauce

Serving: White or brown rice, or Rice Salad with Peas and Soy (Pizza, Pasta & Grains, page 86); Herbed Green Salad with Soy Vinaigrette (Vegetables, page 12)

Index

About the Author

Mark Bittman created and wrote the weekly *New York Times* column "The Minimalist," which ran for thirteen years. He currently covers food policy and all topics related to eating in a weekly op-ed column for the *New York Times*, and is the lead writer for the *Eat* column in the Sunday *New York Times Magazine*.

Bittman has written more than a dozen cookbooks, including *The Minimalist Cooks at Home*, *The Minimalist Cooks Dinner*, *The Minimalist Entertains*, as well as the popular family of kitchen standards *How to Cook Everything*, *How to Cook Everything Vegetarian*, and *How to Cook Everything The Basics*. Bittman explores global cuisines in *The Best Recipes in the World*, an inspired collection of recipes culled from his international travels. With Jean-Georges Vongerichten, he coauthored *Jean-Georges* (winner of a James Beard Award) and *Simple to Spectacular*. And his bestselling *Food Matters* and *Food Matters Cookbook* offer simple ways to improve your diet and the health of the planet.

As a longtime feature on commercial and public television, Bittman has hosted three award-winning cooking series on PBS, is often invited to share his viewpoints on news and magazine programs, and appears regularly on the *Today* show. He also records a weekly web video for the magazine, revisiting recipes from the beloved Minimalist column. For more information, visit www.markbittman.com.

Notes